MW00626049

How to Stop Doubting the Book of Mormon

An ex-Catholic shares an outside perspective of the testament

Chaeli J. Karval

Chaeli J. Karval
Burlington, VT

LCCN: 2021914565

ISBN: 978-0-578-95330-4 (pbk)
ISBN: 978-0-578-95331-1 (ebook)

480e39fc2c52e432b395314b014d1ea97b88717c35
1e2aac73f02891922f1a9e

Contents

Introduction

How Can We Know the Way?

The faith of the Church of Jesus Christ of Latter-day Saints is fundamental to devout believers as the spiritual cornerstone for personality, identity, interpretations of perceptions, thoughts, opinions, self-regulation, reassurance, emotions, and guidance for regulation of family, social groups, and organizations. For the more devout, like the bottom block of a tower, if faith crumbles, all of these effects founded upon it will plummet into disorganized rubble, and the bearer is left with the spiritual crisis of having to construct a new perspective, sometimes from scratch, likely while trying to maintain at least a portion of their daily and social routines and relationships. Questioning faith is risky and dangerous, and doubts can be debilitatingly terrifying for this reason. However, sometimes doubts come to threaten faith uninvited, especially for those who are determined to learn more about what is most important to them. When first acknowledged, these doubts can make us wonder if God is really there, if we really matter, what we are, and why we exist. We try prayer, but it fails to give us the immediate relief that we starve for. We fear that God is disappointed in us for weak faith, and we tend to blame ourselves, because God would not abandon His child without a perfect reason. It can feel as though God is withdrawn from us, because in this state, we struggle to identify His presence. If our loving and merciful God feels this way about us, we think, we must have thought or done some severely wrong things. We are left feeling alone, confused, and perhaps guilty and despairing. Even if our doubts in the faith are mild, ignoring them does not make them go away.

I was never a member of the Church of Jesus Christ of Latter-Day Saints, and I am no expert on their traditions. I was born and raised in the Catholic faith, and indoctrinated into the teachings of a canonically illicit clerical organization called the Society of Saint Pius the Tenth, (SSPX). The SSPX preaches the Catholic faith and it is recognized by the Roman Catholic Church as Catholic. Its distinction from the Roman Catholic Church is its detestation of more modern Catholic culture traceable to a church council, (a series of meetings for church leaders to decide on and proclaim changes or additions to traditions), in the 1960s, as well as its history of disobedience against the

4

authority of the pope, and the Catholic Church's intolerance for their rejection of and disdain for that council. At the time of this writing, the SSPX claims well under a million followers globally, (General statistics about the SSPX, 2020). As a young adult, the conservative Catholic faith of the SSPX was the foundational perspective of every interpretation I made of myself and of my surroundings. To me, the SSPX had the only God, the only good way of thinking and behaving, the only truth, and the only access to true happiness. I believed that even the Roman Catholic Church was a dangerous and questionably valid place to seek goodness.

I am no longer a Catholic. I can trace the loss of my faith back to a single day that I remember well enough when I was 19 years old. It was a Sunday and I was sitting in the choir loft in an SSPX chapel, among the other choir members during the sermon, a routine part of the Catholic Sunday service between the first and second parts of the Mass. While sitting there modestly, whether it was because of the sermon or my wandering mind, I became fully aware of a doubt that I had dismissed so many times before, only this time, I did not dismiss it, nor did I forget about it later. I wondered, if there are approximately seven billion people in the world, how is it that this tiny percentage of people are the only ones with the right way? A question that perhaps should have caused only curiosity threatened my entire reality. How could God command the eternal disposal of nearly everyone dying on the earth at that moment, or at the very least, how could He allow all of these people to live their lives to completion, their only chance to become saints and avoid eternal damnation, without surrounding them with the same opportunity I had of knowing the only right way? How is it that those who choose to follow the SSPX are supposedly the only ones who care enough to seek excellence? How is it that everyone else has not made the effort to discover why we are here on the earth, and what holds more value and durable, continuing happiness than material or momentary pleasure? If people cared about what is important, the SSPX would be honored and followed in every town, government, and household. Is the faith of the SSPX unfairly difficult to believe such that these outsiders do not get a fair chance for salvation, or is it that almost nobody cares about the purpose of their lives such that they do not make an effort to seek information about it, preferring rather to live in lazy ignorance and to only seek to enjoy the temporary pleasures of this mortal life? How are there so many different major religious beliefs, but ours is the only one that happens to be right? How am I so lucky? What if the SSPX is wrong? What if another religion is correct, and we are the ones worshiping a false god? What if nobody has the right religion? What if God does not care about His creation? What if there is no god at all? What if the devil is trying to scare me into seeking alternative explanations so that I sin and displease God, or lose my soul? What if I am having these thoughts and feeling alone because God has left me? I began praying in a frantic attempt to restore my faith and bond with God, but I got stuck addressing God, praying in thoughts like, "whoever you are", and "if you are real", and "even if you are not the eternally loving and interested God I imagine you to be...". At that time, the terror of this doubt was more real to me than my faith, or even my physical surroundings. The immense fear that I could be completely alone in my awareness both among humans and in my universe necessitated concentration to my mind and body to prevent a display of emotional anguish while I was sitting there, leg to leg in that pew with people who I would not dare trust to understand my inner crisis or address it properly. I wanted answers, not criticism or judgment for weak faith, nor reinforcement of their conclusions I could not sustain at that time which would only magnify the feeling that I was alone in my thoughts. I finished my prayer throughout the sermon, the singing, and the remainder of the Mass, begging God to help me find the right answers. I resolved to remember this experience and to seek the truth and only the truth, because I did not want to fail in the eyes of Goodness Itself, nor did I want to feel that immense horror of doubt ever again.

No two crises of faith are the same of course. Sometimes a crisis of faith can come from hardship or grief in life, tempting us to question if God is disinterested or cruel. Sometimes it could simply come from feeling like God is ignoring prayer or effort. It could also come in the form of temptation to sin, or temptations to seek and prioritize things that are less important than God. Regardless, unsettled doubts in the faith are spiritually harmful. Even if we enthusiastically desire to leave the church in pursuit of what the church denies to us or discourages us from, and only hope that our departure brings us no consequence from God, that uncertainty we ignored can haunt or damage us throughout our lives.

While I sought to educate myself to address my doubts in the months following that frightening experience, I remember wishing I had a resource that was brave enough to examine my religion from a perspective pure of simply validating a pre-drawn conclusion. I wanted a resource that would be ready to accept either the conclusion that my church was true or that it was false. Now, after having left the Catholic church, I understand the difficulty of finding such a resource, because in order to create a resource, knowledge must be attained and judged first by the writers, and only written about afterward. However, knowing the value and necessity of an objective perspective, in this book, I will show how I apply it to the Book of Mormon. After years of pondering over Catholic spiritual literature to more deeply understand my faith as a form of worship and self-care, I learned to apply that same method of concentration to other literary material. Although I was never a member of the Church of Jesus Christ of Latter-day Saints, I can provide a perspective which is external to the faith, but also, in a generalized way, internal, because of my spiritual experience as a devout Catholic. Therefore, in this book, I will only provide my perspective on what I have examined, that is, The Book of Mormon, and not on other traditions or literature of the Church of Jesus Christ of Latter-day Saints. Gathering different perspectives together in our mind is helpful in the pursuit of certainty. Burdens of spiritual doubt are not unique to my life story, nor do they uniquely attack the religious beliefs I held.

Before we begin this external look into the Book of Mormon, it is important to prepare with the best mindset for success. So how do we escape from doubts of the faith, and return to God's strength and protection? To purify yourself from doubt, start with God. Remember His perfect love. He understands you better than you understand yourself. If He exists, He provides you with a way to peace. For now, believe at least in the perfect, loving nature of God, even if you struggle to, because we will address that doubt. Next, you will need to recognize and sustain your motivation and desire for truth. The only way to defeat doubt is to confront it, and this process can take a long time. You are going to need to keep reminding yourself of your goal of spiritual peace throughout the process so you can stay motivated. It is easy to feel motivated while immersed in an emotional state that nudges you, but unless you remember and retain the same motivation when you feel more calm, the problem or imperfection remains within you.

It is so important to remember the perfectly good traits of God and to bring Him with you in your heart as you prepare to face your doubts, because the power of God should be sufficient to armor you against the strongest enemy. Jesus said, "I am the way, the truth, and the life", (John 14:6). The Son of God declares that He is truth. This comforting verse provides us with the perfect gateway to spiritual peace because doubt does not threaten the truth. Nothing can, because truth is not flexible. It is solid and unchanging. Therefore, as long as you seek truth, you will be following the way to God without losing Him nor offending Him, and you will escape the storm of doubts.

To face your doubts and find Truth, you will need to understand the importance of thinking objectively. Your feelings and emotions are important to recognize and address, but logical thinking must have the authority in this exploration for truth. If you allow feelings and emotions to make conclusions, you will stray away from the truth, and continue to live with doubt. As you read this book, notice when you feel fear or worry in your mind and body. When those feelings arise, take a second to separate those feelings from your objective analysis, and use your motivation for success to provide reassurance for, and to assert dominance over those feelings. The same applies to feelings of excitement. Excitement for the outcome you are hoping for could influence you into bias. When you feel it arise, redirect your excitement to what you know you can look forward to no matter the outcome: certainty, and celebration in knowing that you bravely sought Truth and peace, and made it to the other side of these haunting doubts.

If the Book of Mormon teaches the truth, it is with God, and it will withstand all your doubts. With this faith, you must bear your cross and continue forward, ready to sacrifice your interpretations of the universe and your identity in order to restore your spiritual life in the truth, whether truth is in the church or elsewhere. Then can you finally rejoice, as we rejoice in the Son of God risen from the dead. Allow doubts to prosecute the Book of Mormon, just as God, knowing His own infinite power, allowed man to put His beloved son on trial, so that He could restore us. Under God, you are the court judge in your own mind, not the prosecutor. Doubts are the prosecution. It is your job to provide your most accurate judgment to the trial. Scholars may defend the Book of Mormon, and unbelievers will challenge it. You are welcome to hear them all, but do not surrender your judgment seat to them in your own mind. Scholars of any topic may have an advantage over most other people with their knowledge, but it is important to remember that scholars are not born that way. They were once students before they became teachers and are still no more nor less human than you are, no matter how much knowledge nor persuasive skill they have, and no matter how stupid or ignorant you believe yourself to be. Use scholars as resources of information and understanding, not as authorities over your own opinions. Your doubts will continue to haunt you until you reach your own conclusions. Retain this mindset, and you are ready for your journey to come closer to Truth.

Chapter 1

I Am

We can test the accuracy of the Book of Mormon by evaluating God within it. Among other descriptors, God is perfect, (Matt. 5:48; 3 Ne. 12:48), unchanging, (Heb. 13:8; Mosiah 2:22; Morm. 9:9, 9:19; Moro. 8:18), omnipotent, (Rev. 1:8, 1 Ne. 7:12; Jacob 2:5; Mosiah 3:5, 17-18, 21, 4:9; Alma 26:35, 44:5; Morm. 5:23; Ether 3:4), and perfectly just, (Acts 10:34; Col. 3:25; Alma 42:22). If we should be loyal to a god who exemplifies these traits, then we will not lose Him by denying a god who contradicts them. By keeping the traits of God in mind, we can remain loyal to Him as we evaluate some of the behaviors of God in the Book of Mormon that could cause doubt. The goal of this chapter is to determine if the god of the Book of Mormon matches the same profile as our God or not, so that we can confront and settle any of these doubts with the truth.

The testament began in ancient Jerusalem. God commanded Lehi to gather his family and depart into the wilderness, which Lehi did, leaving his property behind, (1 Ne. 2:2-4). After having ventured into the wilderness and set up tents, God commanded Lehi's sons to return to Jerusalem to obtain genealogy records from a man named Laban, (1 Ne. 3:14). Lehi's sons obediently returned to Jerusalem. Laban was unwilling to surrender the records, so while he was vulnerable, Nephi, a son of Lehi, killed Laban with God's permission. The Spirit spoke to Nephi:

And it came to pass that I was constrained by the Spirit that I should kill Laban; but I said in my heart: Never at any time have I shed the blood of man. And I shrunk and would that I might not slay him.

And the Spirit said unto me again: Behold the Lord hath delivered him into thy hands. Yea, and I also knew that he had sought to take away mine own life; yea, and he would not hearken unto the commandments of the Lord; and he also had taken away our property.

And it came to pass that the Spirit said unto me again: Slay him, for the Lord hath delivered him into thy hands;

Behold the Lord slayeth the wicked to bring forth his righteous purposes. It is better that one man should perish than that a nation should dwindle and perish in unbelief. (1 Ne. 4:10-13)

Afterward, the sons of Lehi depart Jerusalem and return to the camp in the wilderness, (1 Ne. 5:1). Then, God again commands the sons of Lehi to return to Jerusalem to invite an additional family, the family of Ishmael, on the journey away from Jerusalem, and they obey, (1 Ne. 7:2-3).

Looking at this storyline critically, it was not necessary for the sons of Lehi to depart Jerusalem more than once. Any defenses for this are only speculations that the Book of Mormon is silent about. God knows His plan, and His plan was for Lehi's tribe to depart from Jerusalem with those genealogy records as well as with the family of Ishmael.

The records that God commanded the sons of Lehi to retrieve from Laban rightfully belonged to Laban. The genealogy was also of his ancestry, (1 Ne. 5:16). God's plan allowed these records to be kept in Laban's family rather than in Lehi's, only to be stolen later under His command by condoning the killing of the property owner while he was in a vulnerable state. The killing of Laban was justified by God's perfect nature for the cause of ensuring more believers in the future, as though there was not a more perfect way to do this. An all-powerful god does not need specific brass plates of record to achieve his plan, yet, to God, this was necessary.

God seems to work inefficiency. As we read in the book of Alma, when the prophet Alma arrived in the city of Ammonihah, the people there did not welcome his preaching:

And it came to pass that when Alma had come to the city of Ammonihah he began to preach the word of God unto them.

Now Satan had gotten great hold upon the hearts of the people of the city of Ammonihah; therefore they would not hearken unto the words of Alma.

Nevertheless Alma labored much in the spirit, wrestling with God in mighty prayer, that he would pour out his Spirit upon the people who were in the city; that he would also grant that he might baptize them unto repentance. (Alma 8:8-10)

Despite his mighty prayer, Alma was rejected and harassed until he departed the city. Alma then decided to journey on to preach in the city of Aaron, (Alma 8:11-13). On his journey, while sorrowing over the wickedness of the people in Ammonihah, an angel came to him and commanded him to go back to Ammonihah to preach again, (Alma 8:16). On his return to Ammonihah, Alma meets Amulek who becomes his mission partner, (Alma 8:20, 30). Amulek explains that he also saw an angel who told him of Alma's journey into Ammonihah, and the angel had instructed him to welcome Alma. Amulek obeyed the angel, (Alma 10:7-8). God had a plan for Alma and Amulek to meet prior to preaching in Ammonihah, yet He allowed Alma to experience a failed attempt to preach there first, and did not intervene until after Alma departed from the city. Even if God was only waiting for Alma to ask for help, God did not send the angel to Alma to respond to his mighty prayer. The angel was only sent to explain God's plan when Alma sorrowed after his departure from the city from the failed attempt. Without explanation for this, God's perfection is left questionable for His inefficiency and unjustified delay. God's behavior here is also questionable for changing, because He did not intervene to help, even "wrestling" against His own prophet who was carrying out His will, but after a short time during which the situation remained the same, He intervened to help Alma.

God gave the Jaredites instructions to build imperfect boats. After constructing them, Jared's brother, who received the blueprint from God, asked for guidance on improving the boats:

> And it came to pass that the brother of Jared cried unto the Lord, saying: O Lord, I have performed the work which thou hast commanded me, and I have made the barges according as thou hast directed me.
> And behold, O Lord, in them there is no light; whither shall we steer? And also we shall perish, for in them we cannot breathe, save it is the air which is in them; therefore we shall perish.
> And the Lord said unto the brother of Jared: Behold, thou shalt make a hole in the top, and also in the bottom; and when thou shalt suffer for air thou shalt unstop the hole and receive air. And if it be so that the water come in upon thee, behold, ye shall stop the hole, that ye may not perish in the flood. (Ether 2:18-20)

God waited until Jared's brother presented serious flaws in the boats before He provided the solution. If the Jaredites used these boats on faith alone without asking any questions about the perfect design, it is probable that they could have had to damage them during their voyage, or they would have had to secure the doors open at all times, or they could have suffocated. Even after final completion, God's perfect boat design had holes for ventilation which would remain closed until the passengers suffered for air, but could not be opened if opening them would cause flooding.

God provided Alma with a future location of captives from Ammonihah, (Alma 16:6). By telling people the future, God gave people the opportunity to interfere with natural occurrence, but this verse is even more concerning than that because God told the future of human behavior. This welcomes the question of if this revelation robbed the Lamanites of their free will, or if it introduced the possibility of human interference with God's prophecy. Any possibility of this, no matter how minimal, is a contradiction to the perfect nature of God. Even if it were argued that God was only providing Alma with the most likely future location and not a certainty, literal interpretation does not defend this possibility, because God told the future as a certainty, not as a likely possibility. God also told the future of human behavior when He revealed that people four generations later would sell Him, (3 Ne. 27:32). Again, God did not say that this was likely, but that it will occur. From any angle, these revelations are contradictory to the perfect, all-powerful, unchanging nature of God. An all-powerful God who is perfect should not reduce His power to be inferior to human free will.

God reduced His power to be dependent on compliance of human free will several other times. He commanded Ammon to get the Anti-Nephi-Lehis out of the land in order to keep them safe, (Alma 27:11-12). He relied on humans to keep and preserve records through generations, (Alma 37:1-4, 8-9). He alerted Moroni that the Lamanites were in the wilderness and might commence an attack on the weaker part of Manti, (Alma 43:24). He allowed Alma to write down a prophecy that was not to be revealed until after it is fulfilled, (Alma 45:9), allowing the possibility for this information to be accessed prematurely. He depended on Mormon to obey Him when He forbade him from writing certain things, because He wanted to test the faith of Mormon's people, (3 Ne. 26:11). He allowed babies and newly baptized to say and witness marvelous things that He forbade people from writing down, (3 Ne. 26:16-18). Mormon was forbidden by God from writing the names of those who were spared from experiencing death, (3 Ne. 28:25), and again Mormon was forbidden from writing a full account of things he witnessed, (Morm. 5:9). Moroni was commanded to write with the aim of eradicating evil and the power of Satan from people, (Ether 8:26). Jesus visited the brother of Jared and told him to keep the visit a secret until He, Jesus, glorifies Himself in the flesh. He instead allowed the brother of Jared to write about it in a language that no one else can interpret, and to seal it away with seer stones which will be directly activated or disabled by God, (Ether 3:21-24, 4:1). Although this verse includes a clarification that God will have direct power over the seer stones, it does not solve the problem of the brother of Jared's power to tell others of what he witnessed. A perfect God should not have to require a miracle to protect His secret. Similarly, the chosen disciples are forbidden from talking about certain things that they saw and heard, (3 Ne. 28:14), and although this verse also clarifies that the chosen disciples would not even be permitted to talk about those certain things even if they tried to, this is still a demonstration of imperfection because the perfect method would work without the need for God to contradict the nature He created with the miracle of selective dumbness.

King Lamoni and the missionary Ammon planned a journey to visit King Lamoni's father, who ruled over the whole land as a king, but God told Ammon to not go on this journey because if they did, King Lamoni's father would kill Ammon. God instructs them to make a journey to Middoni instead to rescue Ammon's brothers who have been imprisoned, (Alma 20:1-2). It was therefore God's will that Ammon not encounter, and consequently be killed by, Lamoni's father. It is reasonable to wonder why God was concerned that His will could be contradicted, and why he surrendered this power into Ammon's decision to obey or disobey God. A perfect and all-powerful god does not connect with any possibility of failure against his own will. In obedience to God, Lamoni and Ammon journeyed instead to Middoni. While on their journey, they encountered Lamoni's father, (Alma 20:7-8), which is exactly what God intended to prevent.

God gave prophet Nephi, son of Helaman, supernatural powers including the power to induce famine, pestilence, destruction, and to morph mountains, (Hel. 10:6-10). Nephi, son of Lehi, was also granted a supernatural power which is the power of judgment for the last day, (2 Ne. 33:15). It is completely unnecessary for God to do this. If a prophet can only perform miracles and judgments like these with persistent permission from God, then God is putting extra, unnecessary effort into something He would do on His own anyway, and therefore the gifts become completely useless, and meaningless for the receiver. An all-powerful God who can do an infinite number of simultaneous tasks does not need to bestow supernatural power onto another being, who would need to ask permission to cause miracles anyway. Nephi son of Helaman does exercise his gift by asking God to spare his people from destruction, and to instead punish them with famine. God obeys him, (Hel. 11:4-5), and obeys him again when he asks that the famine be ended, (Hel. 11:12-17). The other possibility is that these gifts of power could counteract against God's will. If Nephi can directly perform miracles, and if Nephi can make judgments for the final day, this would make them gods as they would bypass a need for persistent permission from God to do these things. In this design, Nephi and Nephi could contradict the will of God on a supernatural level. Although God granted these powers in trust and to reward for devotion, humans, unlike God, change their perspectives and adjust their characters throughout their lives, making this a risky decision for God. Whether Nephi and Nephi need persistent permission from God or not to do these things out of their own discernments, neither possibility is a reflection of the perfect nature of God.

The natural man is an enemy of God, (Mosiah 3:19). Even though this verse is referring to man after the sin of Adam, it is still flawed regarding each individual born after Adam's sin. Interpreting this literally, as it should be interpreted, any person born after the sin of Adam is naturally an enemy to God before they do anything. This creates a force which is opposite to God's will for people to be righteous. It is a condition of animosity which the individual has no ability to prevent, meaning that God is deciding that the individual is His enemy without that individual's influence being relevant in the judgment. This is not perfection. It also presents a problem against justice. People are in debt to God because He created life, (Mosiah 2:34). This is unfair because God created mankind of His own desire. Mankind did not need or ask to be created before they existed. We should not be judged as enemies of God nor as in debt to Him without having done anything to cause those circumstances.

Righteousness is defined by belief in the Holy One of Israel, endurance of the crosses of life on Earth, and hatred of the shame of these things, (2 Ne. 9:18). Those who do not get baptized, and those who do not have perfect faith in the Holy One of Israel, cannot inherit the

Kingdom of God and are damned, (2 Ne. 9:23-24). Those who will not believe in the word of Jesus will be condemned, (3 Ne. 26:10). Anyone who denies the works of Christ, or believes that God no longer works by revelation, prophecy, gifts, tongues, healings, the power of the Holy Ghost, or miracles, are criticized and should not expect mercy, (3 Ne. 29:7). No man can be brought to eternal life without having faith in the name of Christ, (Moro. 7:38). Belief should not be tied to righteousness in this way. Righteousness involves having integrity by basing beliefs on a dominantly logical effort.

The righteous establish beliefs in this way rather than basing them on a disregard for the value of things like humanity, in favor of receiving or preserving things of more temporary gratification which are less valuable. Righteousness requires the domination of thought over emotion. The righteous remain loyal to their beliefs in their behavior. For this reason, people who do not believe in the Holy One of Israel could still be righteous. Regardless, God treats people unfairly on the grounds of not believing. Mormon tells of various consequences that the Jews and the Lamanites were threatened with for their unbelief:

And behold, they shall go unto the unbelieving of the Jews; and for this intent shall they go — that they may be persuaded that Jesus is the Christ, the Son of the living God; that the Father may bring about, through his most Beloved, his great and eternal purpose, in restoring the Jews, or all the house of Israel, to the land of their inheritance, which the Lord their God hath given them, unto the fulfilling of his covenant;

And also that the seed of this people may more fully believe his gospel, which shall go forth unto them from the

Gentiles; for this people shall be scattered, and shall become a dark, a filthy, and a loathsome people, beyond the description of that which ever hath been amongst us, yea, even that which hath been among the Lamanites, and this because of their unbelief and idolatry.

For behold, the spirit of the Lord hath already ceased to strive with their fathers; and they are without Christ and God in the world; and they are driven about as chaff before the wind. (Mormon 5:14-16)

God judges people inaccurately. Beyond the fact that He was punished for sin regardless of His innocence, Jesus Christ was also punished for sins that were committed ignorantly, (Mosiah 3:11). God gives particular hatred to the rich for hating poor people, persecuting good people, and for being puffed-up, (2 Ne. 9:30, 42). By doing this, God criticizes people just for being rich. If He wanted to criticize people for hating poor people, persecuting good people, and for being puffed-up, He could make that point without associating wealth to it. Being rich does not directly cause this evil. Some people, when given power, will reveal their evil intentions that they could not reveal before, but the evil itself is not caused by wealth. It is only made more identifiable by the power that comes from wealth. God repeats this error not just against the rich, but also against those who are wise, learned, and those who preach false doctrine, (2 Ne. 9:42, 28:15). Like being rich, being wise, learned, and teaching false doctrine are not condemnable without additional factors. God also unfairly judged those who would refuse to see or hear His counsels, (2 Ne. 9:31-32). This judgment is too vague to be fair. Although in most situations it is probably a good idea to listen, no one should be rebuked

23

simply for not listening. Not listening to the word of God is not an evil action without additional factors that make it evil, such as purposeful disrespect, hatred, or bullying for example. It is possible to refuse to listen to the word of God without having evil disposition. A person might simply feel certain in their own theory of spirituality to the extent that the word of God only appears silly or annoying to them, and such a person can refuse to listen to it without being disrespectful to the messenger. Humans cannot read others' thoughts, so they rely on their observations of behaviors to make judgments. God knows all things, (2 Ne. 9:20), yet according to these examples, He still often judges people dominantly by their actions. He decided that He would no longer accept burnt offerings as sacrifices, (3 Ne. 9:19), indicating that the disposition of the person making the sacrifice is irrelevant. This was also in contradiction to His unchanging nature because He changed His opinion of burnt offerings. God also created conditions which punished innocent people even before they could have been conceived. He cursed the seed of executioners so that any of their offspring would also torture the followers of God, (Mosiah 17:15-19). He similarly cursed the seeds of the priests of Noah, (Alma 25:12).

A series of natural disasters occur in the New World at the time of the crucifixion of Christ. One of these disasters was the covering of the city of Moronihah. God buried the entire city so that He did not have to see the iniquity there, and so that the blood of the prophets and saints could no more come against the people of the city, (3 Ne. 9:5). This is a unique explanation because it does not label the disaster as a punishment. Because the purpose of this destruction was to hide the city from His own sight, God violated justice when He destroyed these people. Not wanting to look at something is not a just reason for destruction like this. This is also a problem because it is out of character for God to address iniquity because of not wanting to look at it, rather than addressing the problem for the reason that He is a just God. God is supposed to be unchanging without any variation.

Although He advocates for equality among people, (Mosiah 23:6-7), God sometimes works by inequality and favoritism. He protected at least three of his chosen disciples from the temptations of Satan, (3 Ne. 28:39). By doing this, God demonstrated that this protection is within His perfection and justice, yet He withheld this protection from others, allowing them to be exposed to temptation from Satan. He was unfair to others when He disregarded the hardness of Amulek's heart. Instead of chastising Amulek or ignoring him as He would do to others, (2 Ne. 9:31-32), God asked Amulek to prepare to welcome a prophet. This was enough to soften Amulek's heart, (Alma 10:6-8). He gave Amulek the power to read thoughts, (Alma 10:17), and did the same for Ammon, (Alma 18:16). True perfection should not be inconsistent, and these findings of inequality and favoritism challenge the claim of God's unchanging nature.

Jesus Christ's bloodshed atones for our sins due to Adam's sin, (Mosiah 3:11). People can only be forgiven and saved from their sins through Christ, (Alma 38:8-9), mankind will perish and all will be fallen and lost without eternal atonement, (Jacob 7:12; Alma 34:9-10), and Jesus Christ must die in order for people to be saved, (Hel. 14:12-15). The requirement for eternal atonement is excessive because the sinful actions that are being atoned for are not eternal. A sinful mental disposition could possibly last for eternity, but Christ's sacrifice does not atone for sinful mental dispositions. It atones for sins, which are actions caused by mental disposition. If He were sacrificed to atone for sinful mental dispositions themselves, then nobody would still be banished to eternal Hell as punishment. Also, Christ's sacrifice was not an eternal event. Christ lives eternally and has infinite characteristics, but He is not being crucified for an eternal amount of time. If He were, justice would never be fulfilled at the completion of the sacrifice, because the sacrifice would never complete, or, if the merits of the sacrifice exist outside of time, humanity before Christ's time would not have had to wait for salvation. It is also completely unnecessary to sacrifice a man's blood in order to penalize for sin. The entire concept of penalizing is imperfect as it applies to offenses against God, because nobody can deprive an all-powerful God. Human societies use penalties because we have limited power unlike God. We can be unfairly deprived by the immorality of others. If the reason for Jesus Christ's sacrifice is to punish humanity for sin, this is also unnecessary because if the goal is for man to be righteous, it would be more perfect and efficient to create a solution that influences people to become more virtuous rather than using punishment. Although it may be somewhat effective for influencing behavior, punishing is an unnecessary and flawed method for helping people to improve their characters, (Gershoff, 2002). Punishment does not erase the cause of the unwanted behavior. In response to successful punishment, the punished person suppresses the behavior in order to avoid the punishment in the future, and their character remains unreformed without being

26

exposed to different types of influence or learning. The sacrifice of Jesus Christ is not even an effective punishment for the sins of mankind because the physical event of the punishment is isolated to the person, time, and place of Jesus Christ's suffering and death. It is not dealt to the individual sinner immediately following their unwanted behavior. The bloodshed of Jesus Christ is also deemed necessary for God's forgiveness. Forgiveness would mean for God to recognize that a person has the potential to reform their character, and to welcome this potential. A perfect, all-knowing and all-powerful God would forgive by default null of any form of effort. God also shows His limitations for forgiving certain sins, (Alma 39:5-9). Bloodshed does not prove anything to God who knows the nature of mankind better than we know ourselves, especially bloodshed from Jesus Christ who is of God. Regardless of the sacrifice of Jesus Christ, people can still be condemned to Hell, so the sacrifice does not solve the problem of trust either, because those who are sent to Hell are sent there because God does not trust them in His presence, or to ever become better. By these deductions, God is left without a reason for requiring the bloodshed of Jesus Christ. God is a condemner, and He is given praise for saving people from His own wrath, (Alma 26:13-17; 2 Ne. 9:19). This hero-like status contradicts itself, and therefore, it is imperfect. God also uses His voluntary and unnecessary sacrifice of His son to exploit repentance and submission out of people, (3 Nephi 9:22). The Book of Mormon defends God with the perspective that God atones for the sins of the world so that He can be both perfectly just and also merciful, (Alma 42:23-25). This defense is contradicted in both directions for this all-powerful God. It is God's own

27

justice that requires Christ to pay for the debt of sin in order to gain access to His own power of forgiveness to save sinners, and it is also His own capacity to forgive that requires Him to deprive mankind from their just punishments by unjustly placing them on an innocent man. Either way, perfect forgiveness or justice is contradicted. Ironically, this problem is acknowledged when Alma spoke to his son Corianton:

Therefore, according to justice, the plan of redemption could not be brought about, only on conditions of repentance of men in this probationary state, yea, this preparatory state; for except it were for these conditions, mercy could not take effect except it should destroy the work of justice.
Now the work of justice could not be destroyed; if so, God would cease to be God. (Alma 42:13).

God understands that His mercy is limited because unlimited mercy would require Him to work against His form of justice, but the claim here is that if people repent, then justice will not be violated by mercy. This is not true because even though some people repent, allowing God to be both merciful and just, God still requires the bloody sacrifice of Jesus for all of mankind regardless. Repentance is useless to God without the sacrifice of Jesus Christ. Not only does God fail to achieve perfect forgiveness, but when He does achieve forgiveness, He continues to require effort to sustain that forgiveness that was already established, (Mosiah 4:12). If forgiveness needs to be sustained, then the sins were never actually forgiven. Jesus Christ was also crucified in God's plan to draw more people to Himself, (3 Ne. 27:14-15), as though there could not have been a more perfect and efficient way for God to achieve this.

28

God used the method of punishment regularly. By using punishment to influence people, God demonstrates His failure to understand that it is not the perfect way. He punished the people of Zeniff with famine because they were slow to remember him, (Mosiah 9:3). His solution for discouraging iniquity and unbelief among the Nephites was to destroy them with wars and pestilence, (Alma 45:10-12). He punished iniquity with a curse of disappearing tools, (Ether 14:1). The people of Ammonihah were threatened with severe destruction because of their persistence in wickedness, because God would rather destroy His people than allow them to live in wickedness, (Alma 9:18-19). If God would prefer that His people are given salvation above all other possible outcomes, then by this rationalization, He is settling for a lesser goal, because He has the power and knowledge to influence people to change.

There are additional examples of God's preference for punishment, but the entire concept of Hell is the most concerning example. Hell is eternal punishment for those who die without forgiveness from God for their sins. Hell is referred to in 2 Ne. 2:29, 26:10, and 28:15, Jacob 3:11 and 6:10, and in Mosiah 2:38-39 and 3:25-27. Even if the fear of Hell deters sin while a person is alive, after death, the eternal punishment is useless because it lasts forever, preventing any possibility or usefulness for character reform. This is a problem against perfect justice because useless punishment is not fair or good for anyone. Hell is a problem because sinners are punished eternally for sins that were not eternally depriving against righteousness, nor were their sins nonredeemable or noncorrectable.

God's preference for punishment has consequences that go against His will. God commands people to repent, be baptized in His name, and to have perfect faith in Him, or else they will not inherit the kingdom of God. Those who do not do these things will be damned. However, those who do not know the law of God will be delivered from damnation, (2 Ne. 9:23-28). It is better to remain ignorant without baptism than to be baptized and then deny God, (2 Ne. 31:14), and it would be better to not be born than to hear the word of God but not hearken to it, (3 Ne. 28:34-35). After having been enlightened by the Spirit of God, but then falling away into sin and transgression, people become worse off than they would have been if they had remained ignorant, (Alma 24:30). This system presents a concerning flaw in God's perfect nature. Under this system, a guaranteed way to be spared from damnation is to remain ignorant of the law of God. Even though someone can also be spared from damnation through faith and obedience, if learning of the law of God exposes someone to the possibility of damnation, it is wisest to remain ignorant if the goal is salvation. Even if God does not save those who intentionally remain ignorant, this system is still imperfect because people could intentionally withhold the law of God from the ignorant people in order to protect them from damnation, and toward that altruistic goal, it would still be wiser to protect the ignorance of these people than to teach them of the law of God.

Man is given the free will to choose between either freedom and eternal life, or captivity and eternal death, according to the power of the devil, (2 Ne. 2:27, 10:23). This is incorrect because nobody would freely choose captivity and eternal death. If God wants to offer man the free will to choose eternal life, He cannot manipulate this choice by restricting man to the threat of captivity and death as the only alternative. This is known as holding victims under duress, and the victims' choice would not be considered free. Nephi's free will was also directly violated when the Spirit constrained him to speak, (2 Ne. 28:1), and Jared's brother was chastised by God for not praying, (Ether 2:14).

When you are serving others, you are only in service to the Lord, (Mosiah 2:17). If God wants us to love others, this is not the perfect perspective to have, nor the perfect method of encouraging it. A person who does good for others only because they want to serve the God who will determine their destination in the afterlife, does not need to have empathy for others. Just because a person does something kind for someone else does not mean that they are doing it virtuously. This imperfect method allows a loophole for people who are only acting out of self-interest or perhaps out of fear. Someone who serves others out of a charitable understanding that those other people have minds and lives as vivid as their own would directly and perfectly fulfill God's will for people to serve others.

After the series of natural disasters occur in the New World in association with the time of the crucifixion of Christ, the voice of God is heard throughout the land, and declares that those who survived the natural disasters were more righteous than those who were killed, so that He could offer His mercy to the more righteous, (3 Ne. 9:13-14). The survivors had lamented and howled in their grief for the loss of their loved ones, (3 Ne. 10:2). People do not desire to endure grief, and sometimes people would rather not survive severe tragedy like this. God saw himself as merciful for allowing these people to survive even though they could not feel happy in their grief. God focused on offering His mercy to the righteous rather than offering it to the people who lived in wickedness, who needed God's mercy more than the righteous. Had God spared the wicked, He could have offered them His mercy because as long as people are alive, we know that they have the potential to improve their characters. An all-knowing God would know the nature of humans better than humans understand themselves, and He also knows what can be done to influence people to change for the better. If the wicked did not even have the potential to improve themselves, then they did not have free will. A perfect god would not kill people just to penalize or punish them if he also wanted them to have free will and to help them amend their sinful tendencies.

Regardless of God's intolerance for iniquity, God requires human iniquity in His design. It was God's design for Adam to eat the forbidden fruit so that man could know good from evil, and so that God could redeem mankind from sin:

And now, behold, if Adam had not transgressed he would not have fallen, but he would have remained in the garden of Eden. And all things which were created must have remained in the same state in which they were after they were created; and they must have remained forever, and had no end.

And they would have had no children; wherefore they would have remained in a state of innocence, having no joy, for they knew no misery; doing no good, for they knew no sin.

But behold, all things have been done in the wisdom of him who knoweth all things.

Adam fell that men might be; and men are, that they might have joy.

And the Messiah cometh in the fulness of time, that he may redeem the children of men from the fall. And because that they are redeemed from the fall they have become free forever, knowing good from evil; to act for themselves and not to be acted upon, save it be by the punishment of the law at the great and last day, according to the commandments which God hath given. (2 Ne. 2:22-26)

Again, God's will for Adam's disobedience is revealed in the book of Alma:

For behold, if Adam had put forth his hand immediately, and partaken of the tree of life, he would have lived forever, according to the word of God, having no space for repentance; yea, and also the word of God would have been void, and the great plan of salvation would have been frustrated.

But behold, it was appointed unto man to die – therefore, as they were cut off from the tree of life they should be cut off from the face of the earth – and man became lost forever, yea, they became fallen man.

And now, ye see by this that our first parents were cut off both temporally and spiritually from the presence of the Lord; and thus we see they became subjects to follow after their own will.

Now behold, it was not expedient that man should be reclaimed from this temporal death, for that would destroy the great plan of happiness.

Therefore, as the soul could never die, and the fall had brought upon all mankind a spiritual death as well as a temporal, that is, they were cut off from the presence of the Lord, it was expedient that mankind should be reclaimed from this spiritual death.

Therefore, as they had become carnal, sensual, and devilish, by nature, this probationary state became a state for them to prepare; it became a preparatory state.

And now remember, my son, if it were not for the plan of redemption, (laying it aside) as soon as they were dead their souls were miserable, being cut off from the presence of the Lord.

And now, there was no means to reclaim men from this fallen state, which man had brought upon himself because of his own disobedience;... (Alma 42:5-12)

Interpreting this literally, God wanted Adam to disobey Him. God planned for mankind to fall so that He could be a hero. God wanted mankind to know good from evil, even though He forbade them from eating that fruit. Because of this, mankind became carnal, sensual, and devilish by nature, and the blame was placed on mankind. In accordance with God's plan, mankind became in debt to God for doing wrong, even though that was exactly what God wanted. God also took credit for the gift of free will through the redemption, (2 Ne. 2:27), even though according to these excerpts above, man gained access to free will simply by Adam's disobedience.

God chose to send Jesus Christ to live among the Jews because no other nation would crucify their God, and then he declared that He will punish the Jewish people for their iniquities that would lead to the crucifixion:

Wherefore, as I said unto you, it must needs be expedient that Christ— for in the last night the angel spake unto me that this should be his name— should come among the Jews, among those who are the more wicked part of the world; and they shall crucify him— for thus it behooveth our God, and there is none other nation on earth that would crucify their God.

For should the mighty miracles be wrought among other nations they would repent, and know that he be their God.

But because of priestcrafts and iniquities, they at Jerusalem will stiffen their necks against him, that he be crucified.

Wherefore, because of their iniquities, destructions, famines, pestilences, and bloodshed shall come upon them; and they who shall not be destroyed shall be scattered among the nations. (2 Ne. 10:3-6)

God could have punished the Jews for their iniquities without presenting Jesus Christ to them. Instead, God used the iniquity of the Jews with a plan for Jesus Christ's crucifixion, and then punished the Jews for it. This is a contamination against justice. God's action of pre-planning Jesus Christ's death makes Him just as guilty as He deems the Jews to be for the crucifixion. God directly contradicted Himself by punishing the Jews for His own behavior. For these reasons, God can not be compatible with a god who is perfect, all-powerful, unchanging, or perfectly just.

The Lamanites were given a curse of dark skin due to the transgressions from righteousness by their ancestry. This was God's way of protecting His people from believing in incorrect traditions, (Alma 3:6-9). The perfect and all-powerful method for influencing people to not believe something would not involve punishment without positive reinforcement. If there was positive reinforcement to go along with this curse, it should have been at least just as important, just as customized, and just as documented in the scripture for this story as the punishment, but nothing for that is mentioned. This method is also flawed because in order for it to work, the righteous Nephites have to believe that breeding with someone who has dark skin is a bad idea. If the

Nephites were to not see this as a problem, the curse would have become meaningless. God did the same thing to the Amlicites, (Alma 3:13-15).

Korihor, an atheist, was brought before Alma for preaching in disagreement with the church, (Alma 30:29-30). Alma was serving the land as chief judge and governor at that time. Alma interviewed Korihor and determined that he was a threat for presenting a danger to the faith of the people. Korihor stated that he would not believe in God without a sign, but Alma declared that Korihor's requirement for a sign should not be satisfied:

> And now Korihor said unto Alma: If thou wilt show me a sign that I may be convinced that there is a God, yea, show unto me that he hath power, and then will I be convinced of the truth of thy words.
>
> But Alma said unto him: Thou hast had signs enough; will ye tempt your God? Will ye say, Show unto me a sign, when ye have the testimony of all these thy brethren, and also all the holy prophets? The scriptures are laid before thee, yea, and all things denote there is a God; yea, even the earth, and all things that are upon the face of it, yea, and its motion, yea, and also all the planets which move in their regular form do witness that there is a Supreme Creator. (Alma 30:43-44)

Miracles are not performed as evidence of God for those doubters who can notice the life-sustaining nature of the universe, or for those doubters who have heard people preaching of God. If a request for a sign from God is assumed to be a bluff for not wanting the obligation to obey the laws of God, this is poor judgment because it is possible for a person to notice the nature of the universe and hear preaching of God, yet not have enough reason to conclude that the God of the Book of Mormon is real. However, there is a bigger problem here because at the time of Jesus Christ's death, many miraculous signs were performed for the intent that there will be no cause for unbelief among people, (Hel. 14:28). God provides signs for people to believe, yet He also denies them to Korihor for the same reason. This is not characteristic of an unchanging God.

After explaining these reasons for denying signs to those who doubt, Alma warned Korihor that if he were to deny God one more time, he would be struck dumb by God, (Alma 30:47). Korihor reaffirms his requirement for a sign in order to believe, and Alma responds by declaring that Korihor is to become dumb as he had warned, and that this would be a sign of God's existence for Korihor. At this, Korihor was struck dumb, (Alma 30:48-50). By this story, we can interpret that God wanted to protect the people from the false teachings of Korihor instead of trusting the truth to be sufficient to protect itself. Truth welcomes critical thought because critical thinking is directed toward knowledge of truth and therefore does not threaten it. Another problem with this story is that although Korihor was found unworthy to be given a sign of God, in continuing his unwelcomed behavior, he was eventually given the sign that he was initially denied. This is a contradiction to God's perfect nature because although the intent was to establish that Korihor's behavior was undeserving of a sign, Korihor's behavior was ultimately encouraged when he got a sign which he required. In psychology, this sequence imitates a fixed-ratio schedule, (Ferster and Skinner, 1957 and 1997). A fixed-ratio schedule is a type of intermittent reinforcement schedule. Intermittent reinforcement schedules mean that a behavior is reinforced, but not every time it is performed. This is in contrast with a continuous reinforcement schedule which reinforces the behavior every time it is performed. The fixed-ratio schedule reinforces a behavior only after a fixed number of times that the behavior occurs. In this case, the encouraged behavior is Korihor's statements of his requirement of a sign in order to believe. Once the actor learns to continue the behavior, a fixed-ratio schedule reinforces the behavior more strongly than continuous reinforcement schedules do because once the reinforcement factor is removed, in a fixed-ratio schedule, the behavior continues more before it extinguishes in contrast with the behavior in a continuous reinforcement schedule. In more simple terms, if a person understands that they have to do something a certain number of times to get what they want, they will have more patience for results than someone who has learned to expect to get what they want every time they make an effort for it. Against the will of God, this would make unbelievers more likely to persist in their pursuit of signs of God regardless of being denied them. Also, God's unchanging nature is contradicted in this occurrence because the sign was denied initially, but was then granted in response to the same behavior, and Korihor became no more worthy of that sign between his statements. Even though the sign for Korihor was also punishment, a factor of encouragement should not have been present because that makes it an imperfection. As a punishment, Korihor's sign was dealt to him unfairly. Korihor was not judged as guilty of threatening people, but for threatening faith. Control over faith and belief lies within the individual, not with other people such as

Korihor. Korihor, like anyone else, could not control people's minds, and he was not sentenced to become dumb for any other reason than stating what he believed and why. The story of Korihor is closed with the devil being blamed for dragging people like this into Hell, (Alma 30:60). It is confusing to use the word "drag" here because that implies that people like this do not want to go to Hell, and that they are taken there as victims. This can lead us to doubt free will, and the justice of God for giving eternal punishment to someone who was only a victim.

There is another story with the same synopsis as the one of the story of Korihor. A man named Sherem preaches against Christ among Nephites. Sherem seeks Jacob in order to challenge his beliefs. The Spirit enters Jacob as an advisor to help him defend Christ, (Jacob 7:8). Like Korihor, Sherem asked for a sign so that he could believe in Christ, but he was shamed for asking for the sign, and then punished with a sign for asking for one by being delivered a blow from God that made him fall to the ground, (Jacob 7:13-15). As with the story of Korihor, instead of allowing Sherem to challenge the strength of truth, Sherem's arguments were taken as a threat. Just for proposing his beliefs and asking for contrary evidence, Sherem was called a devil and was punished, yet by the same consequence, he received his sign that he was just denied. Both Korihor and Sherem were denied what God recognized and agreed to be beneficial for preventing unbelief, (Hel. 14:28).

Not only do all of these contradictions give us understandable causes to doubt that God in the Book of Mormon is our perfect, all-powerful, unchanging, and perfectly just God, but they also give us a confusingly different profile of God that should not be ignored.

Reviewing this examination cynically, the God of the Book of Mormon is neglectful, disinterested in strengthening His children spiritually, rancorous, apathetic, egocentric, exploitative, and oppressive to free thought. His neglect and apathy is shown by his inefficiency, delay, and varying interest in the spiritual welfare of His children. His disinterest is shown from His invitation for failure in His plan, and His failure to give full effort and omnipotent power towards His plan. He is rancorous by judging his children as enemies before they are capable of sin. His exploitative ego is shown by His need and forceful demand for recognition. All of this is shown by a god who claims to be the same entity as God who is love, (John 4:8, 16). These traits would make God hypocritical for claiming to love His children while acting to the contrary. Seeing this dishonesty, God seems to exploit people's spirits and oppress people's free thought. With this plausibility in mind, we encounter the doubt of God's trustworthiness that alludes us to examine how the Book of Mormon values and guides us on how we should use faith. How do we know we can trust that this God knows what is best for us and offers the best to us perfectly at all times, even when His behavior makes it seem like He is not trustworthy?

Chapter 2

The Way

Faith is trust in something as truth without proof. When we decide that we believe something is true, we should be making our best guess. Every belief requires at least a little bit of faith. Faith is not a bad thing, but it is essential. Faith allows us to be satisfied with our best guess of what the truth is, so that we can live our lives efficiently. Without faith, we would not be able to progress beyond pondering to making decisions and taking actions. However, faith should not replace pondering. It is important to seek evidence first, determine which possible truth has the strongest evidence, and only then, reduce the gap between evidence and proof, with faith. Once the belief is established, faith communicates with emotion. Faith is what tells the believer that they are welcome to become attached to those beliefs that they trust, and to emote from the perspective of that truth. Hope is the desire for a specific outcome, based on a perceived possible truth, even if it is not the most likely truth. It is important to keep these elements in order. Faith should not come before evidence and cognition because a faith that is placed first will filter or prevent thinking. Emotion should be submissive to logical thought because if emotion contaminates the gathering of evidence and the pondering over possible truths, then the believer is likely to believe something that would not have been their best guess of what is true, otherwise. Believing in something simply based on what the believer wants to be true is a gamble that can cause emotional pain in the future when reality exposes problems with such beliefs. Strong hope must be submissive to logical thinking because the bearer should be prepared for the most likely outcome, regardless of which outcome they hope for. Strength of hope is not a factor in the likelihood of an outcome. This examination will test the Book of Mormon on the proper use of faith.

Faith is used incorrectly when it asserts belief without having provided evidence or reasoning to support that belief. Some of the fundamental claims of the Book of Mormon are fed to readers to be believed as truths without having provided superior evidence, reasoning, nor pondering in comparison to other possibilities. Nephi wrote that without Christ, there is no God, (2 Ne. 11:7), implying that Christ is necessary for God to exist in the way that He does, but there is no thorough thought sequence provided to support this conclusion. The Book of Mormon provides its own definition of righteousness. All that is good comes from God and all that is evil comes from the devil, (Moro. 7:16-17, 10:25). The righteous are defined by their belief in the Holy one of Israel, that He endured the crosses of the world, and that the shame of this must be despised, (2 Ne. 9:18). The scripture claims that Church services were led by the Holy Ghost, (Moro. 6:9), but there is no logical reason given to show how this conclusion was made. According to God, those who believe that little children should be baptized deserve Hell, (Moro. 8:14, 20-21). People are not to have more than one wife, have concubines, nor commit whoredoms, (Jacob 2:27-28; 3:5-6). Jacob warns his people against sins including fornication and lasciviousness, (Jacob 3:12). Corianton went after a harlot, and this was deemed as a sin only less bad than the shedding of innocent blood and denial of the Holy Ghost, (Alma 39:3-5). None of these baseless claims are given in the scripture with thoughtful explanation. Along with all the miracle claims in the testament, they are expected to be believed to fulfill the requirement of perfect faith for salvation. Whether or not these sins are actually harmful or morally wrong is not the main flaw with these claims. The main concern is that these claims demanded obedience before explanations were provided to support them. This sets the reader up for confirmation bias. Confirmation bias occurs when a person chooses what they believe, and then afterward, only seeks explanations to confirm their belief while ignoring or rejecting any explanations that contradict it.

The Book of Mormon practices confirmation bias because it does not welcome challenges to its claims. People that believe in the word of God and are baptized without being stubborn, and do this without being brought to know the word of God nor compelled to know it beforehand, are blessed, (Alma 32:16). Alma discourages people from asking for signs in order to believe. He promotes faith as something that should be dominant over knowledge, (Alma 32:17-19). Nephi confidently declared that anyone who believes in Christ will believe in what he has to say, without thoroughly or even vaguely explaining why this is certain, (2 Ne. 33:10-11). Ammon praised the queen of the Land of Ishmael for having better faith than the Nephites when she declared that the only support for her faith was Ammon's preachings, (Alma 19:9-10). Faith in Christ is required before He answers any questions about whether something is true or not, (Moro. 10:4). Faith is also commanded in Mosiah 4:11.

The proper order of knowledge before faith is persistently and directly contradicted. Lehi's miraculous compass had words on it that would change based on the faith of the Nephites, (1 Ne. 16:29), therefore withholding information until faith would be achieved. It is assumed that people who deny the revelations and miracles either do not know the gospel of Christ, or they do not understand it, (Morm. 9:7-8), establishing that genuine disbelief after being aware of the teachings is not a possibility. As shown from the story of Korihor, people who know the word of God but claim that they do not believe it are lying, and may be working for the devil to lead people to destruction, (Alma 30:42). To paint this picture that the church of Christ knows obvious truths, the Book of Mormon tells of peoples who unanimously believed in them. Of an entire population of Nephites, every person believed in the faith of the church, (3 Ne. 5:1). This was also true among the Nephites in the year 36 AD, (4 Ne. 1:2). In 3 Ne. 7:18, it was impossible for anyone to not believe Nephi's words only because his faith was strong. Knowledge of the mysteries of God are given to those who already have faith, (Alma 26:22). To safeguard the improper order of faith before knowledge against those who ask for evidence in order to believe, scripture and observation of the physical realm are labeled as sufficient evidence for faith in the teachings of Christ as we learned from the story of Korihor, (Alma 30:44). If this reasoning is following the proper use of faith, miracles and the teachings of Christ are ascertained to be the most reasonable possible truth based on testimony of people and observation of natural science, or even based on the precondition of certainty that there is a supreme creator. The possibility of false testimony in scripture, explanations for physical science that contradict the teachings of Christ, or the possibility of a supreme creator who is not the Christian God are forcibly dismissed as less likely possibilities than miracles. Miracles would be a greatly effective way to provide people with evidence to support the scriptures, but this method does not work and the church knows this, so the scripture provides the stories of Sherem and Korihor as a protection against those who demand proof.

People are discouraged from believing that they are wise. "Wo unto the wise in their own eyes and prudent in their own sight!", (2 Ne. 15:21). It is possible for someone to think that they are wise, pure of incorrectly believing this based on vanity. By this discouragement, people are not only enforced to think that they are not wise, but shamed for ever believing that one day they could be. Obedience to this causes people to disable their abilities of pondering and reasoning when it comes to the teachings within the book because those abilities are interpreted as vanity. These people are forced to skip to faith and hope. Then, because they are offered a way to gain the honorable title of "saint" through submission and meekness, (Mosiah 3:19), followers refrain from challenging the teachings of Christ. In seeking knowledge, people are persuaded to place faith before knowledge, because knowledge is offered as a reward for believing first, (Ether 4:11, 12:6). Wisdom is instead equated with unregulated fear, and only then it is encouraged:

Behold, will ye reject these words? Will ye reject the words of the prophets; and will ye reject all the words which have been spoken concerning Christ, after so many have spoken concerning him; and deny the good word of Christ, and the power of God, and the gift of the Holy Ghost, and quench the Holy spirit, and make a mock of the great plan of redemption, which hath been laid for you?

Know ye not that if ye will do these things, that the power of the redemption and the resurrection, which is in Christ, will bring you to stand with shame and awful guilt before the bar of God?

And according to the power of justice, for justice cannot be denied, ye must go away into that lake of fire and brimstone, whose flames are unquenchable, and whose smoke ascendeth up forever and ever, which lake of fire and brimstone is endless torment.

O then, my beloved brethren, repent ye, and enter in at the strait gate, and continue in the way which is narrow, until ye shall obtain eternal life.

O be wise; what can I say more?

Finally, I bid you farewell, until I shall meet you before the pleasing bar of God, which bar striketh the wicked with awful dread and fear. Amen. (Jacob 6:8-13)

This is the exception where wisdom is advertised as something to strive to have. According to this excerpt, a person is described as wise to believe in Christ to appease the fear of Hell, even when the only rationale to support belief in Christ is testimony. Without strong rationale, this fear is not wisdom, but an emotion taking control. Emotion should always be submissive to rationale for the proper use of faith.

The Book of Mormon advertises and rewards faith in the belief of the church. God will bless and prosper those who follow His commandments, (Mosiah 2:22). Anyone who believes in Christ without any doubt will be able to do and get anything which is pleasing to Him that they ask for, as long as they believe that they will receive it, (Enos 1:15, Morm. 9:21, Moro. 7:26, 7:33, 10:23). God only works by the faith of His children, (2 Ne. 27:23). Repentance is rewarded with prosperity, (Hel. 4:15). With strong and steady enough faith, mountains, trees, or waves will obey us in the name of Jesus, but these signs are withheld from people until that faith is achieved, (Jacob 4:6-7). God promised Zoram that his children will prosper forever until they stop following the commandments of the Lord, (2 Ne. 1:31). For those who obtain hope in Christ, they will gain riches if they intend to use their riches to help the needy, (Jacob 2:19). The people of Nephi became rich because of their prosperity in Christ, (4 Ne. 1:23). Mighty prayer was rewarded with success for the Nephites in battle against the Lamanites and the Amlicites, (Alma 2:28). The power to judge governors on their submission to the faith, and the discretion to fight them if they do not submit to it is granted directly from God to Moroni, a Nephite military commander, (Alma 60:33). A rebellion against the government may have been justifiable for solving hunger, as Moroni threatened in Alma 60:35, but Moroni's actions do not change the meaning of God's word, which granted to him the power to punish the governors simply if they did not repent. God told Enos that it was because of his faith in Christ whom he had never seen nor heard that his guilt was swept away, (Enos 1:8), and granted to Enos and his fathers what they asked for because of their faith, (Enos 1:12, 1:18). Angels appear and minister to people because of faith so reliantly that if this is not happening, it is because of unbelief, (Moro. 7:37). Alma and Amulek remained unharmed within a prison when an earthquake occurred that collapsed the walls of the prison, and this protection was attributed to their faith in Christ, (Alma 14:28). King Lamoni experienced a death-like sleep while he was carried to rest in God to cleanse him from unbelief and to bring joy to his soul, (Alma 19:5-6). Missionaries were granted unhindered access to homes, (Alma 23:1-2). After expressing his disappointment over the Zoramites, Alma clapped his hands over those around him. At this, they were filled with the Holy Ghost, and they were given strength that they would not suffer unless the suffering would be swallowed up in the joy of Christ. These blessings were attributed to Alma's faith, (Alma 31:36-38). Helaman's army won a battle without losing any men, in contrast to their opposition, the Lamanites, who lost 1,000 men in the same battle. Helaman attributed their victory to faith, (Alma 57:25-26). Moroni and Pahorian battled their forces against the Lamanites and won possession of the city of Nephihah without one death among their own people, yet many Lamanites were slain, (Alma 62:26). The Lamanites were rewarded for their righteousness with time and increasing reproduction, (Hel. 7:23-24). Recall that righteousness is based on God's definition, which is belief in Him, (2 Ne. 9:18). Nephi is rewarded with eternal blessing, strength, and supernatural powers for declaring God's word to the people, (Hel. 10:4-10). God praised the brother of Jared for his great faith, and he was rewarded with visions of God, (Ether 3:9-13). Three Nephite disciples are granted protection from both physical and emotional suffering, and a promise of joy in the kingdom of God, (3 Ne. 28:7-10). Disciples of Jesus are rescued from persecution by imprisonment, and suffering from being held in deep pits, a den of wild beasts, and a furnace, by using the power of the word of God, (3 Ne. 28:19-22). If these rewards for faith are taken away, it is because of unbelief, (Moro. 10:24). If you believe on the Son of God, you will have everlasting life, (2 Ne. 25:13, Hel. 14:8). If you obey the spirit of God, you can expect eternal happiness, but if you obey the alternative which is a bad spirit, you can expect eternal misery, (Alma 3:26). Obedience can surrender logical thought to a master, establishing a faith without the individual's own thinking being used, especially when a reward is offered, or when a punishment is threatened.

Those who do not believe should expect consequences. Perfect faith in Christ and baptism are required in order to avoid eternal damnation. Those who do not believe, or reject the word of God, will be damned to Hell, (2 Ne. 9:23, Jacob 6:8-10, Ether 4:18, Moro 7:38). The wise, learned, rich, those puffed up with pride, those who preach false doctrine, those who commit whoredomes, and those who pervert the way of the Lord will go to Hell, (2 Ne. 28:15). Amulek urges people to not procrastinate their repentance at the risk of a state of eternal wickedness:

And now, as I said unto you before, as ye have had so many witnesses, therefore, I beseech of you that ye do not procrastinate the day of your repentance until the end; for after this day of life, which is given us to prepare for eternity, behold, if we do not improve our time while in this life, then cometh the night of darkness wherein there can be no labor performed.

Ye cannot say, when ye are brought to that awful crisis, that I will repent, that I will return to my God. Nay, ye cannot say this; for that same spirit which doth possess your bodies at the time that ye go out of this life, that same spirit will have power to possess your body in that eternal world.

For behold, if ye have procrastinated the day of your repentance even until death, behold, ye have become subjected to the spirit of the devil, and he doth seal you his; therefore, the Spirit of the Lord hath withdrawn from you, and hath no place in you, and the devil hath all power over you; and this is the final state of the wicked. (Alma 34:33-35)

This threat of Hell places importance on changing the possessing spirit rather than placing importance on examining the dispositions and existence of the spirits, or pondering claims over what should or should not be called good behavior. Our free will should grant us the choice to remain free from possession by any spirit. If we are always possessed by one spirit or the other, we have no free will. Free will is necessary to maintain the proper order of thought before faith. Thought is controlled and repentance is enforced when compliance is claimed to be the only alternative to a state of eternal wickedness.

Once people are made aware of the threat of eternal damnation, threats that are vague or unspecified become just as serious. Nephi implies a threat from God when he preaches that those who deny God after baptism would be better off never getting baptized, (2 Ne. 31:14). He threatens non-believers by speaking of "the last day". He bids them "an everlasting farewell" for the condemnation they will have, and declares that whatever he seals on earth will be brought against them on the last day, (2 Ne. 33:11, 14-15). For those who do not hearken to the word of Jesus, "...[I]t would be better for them if they had not been born", (3 Ne. 28:35). Unbelievers will be accursed and deprived of being shown great things by God, and threatened with judgment on the last day, (Ether 4:8-10). God threatens those who deny His revelations, and those who say that He no longer works by revelation, prophecy, gifts, tongues, healings, the power of the Holy Ghost, or miracles by associating them with those who proclaim their disbelief in miracles for attention or personal benefit, and then threatens the latter by saying that they will receive no mercy, (3 Ne. 29:6-7). Mormon threatened the unbelievers by asking them if they will continue to disbelieve when they stand before God, (Morm. 9:2). The book of Mosiah subtly threatened Hell by assuring that a time will come when everyone of every nation will recognize the judgment of God as just, (Mosiah 16:1).

Eternal damnation is not the only consequence for not believing. We know that Korihor was punished with dumbness for declaring his unbelief, and God is consistently aggressive against doubters and unbelievers. The Jews were sentenced to be scourged by other nations until they would believe in Christ, (2 Ne. 25:16). Part of the reason the Lamanites and their seed were given a dark skin was to discourage belief in incorrect traditions, (Alma 3:8). This was a threat against anyone who could explore those beliefs, and it was interference against conclusions that could otherwise be achieved purely cognitively. Those who already have the faith are made to keep it, under the threat of worsened quality of life, (Alma 24:30). This flaw allows believers to have faith just because of fear rather than thought, but this fear is an emotion, so it should not dominate thought. Alma implied that those who place knowledge before faith are cursed, (Alma 32:17-19). Alma exhorted the people of Helam for their fear of the Lamanites and told them that they should remember God and they would be delivered from the Lamanites, (Mosiah 23:25-27). When His voice was being heard throughout the land, God allowed guilt as a deterrent against not believing. He said, "Behold, for such I have laid down my life, and have taken it up again; therefore repent, and come unto me ye ends of the earth, and be saved", (3 Ne. 9:22). Here, He implied that humans are responsible for God's suffering, and that we owe Him whatever He asks for because of it. God chastened the brother of Jared for not remembering to pray, because not remembering to pray is an evil sin, (Ether 2:14-15).

God extends the vitality of hope with intermittent reinforcement schedules. Remember, an intermittent reinforcement schedule means that a behavior is not rewarded every time it is performed. In this case, the behavior is faith. Enos prayed to God for a whole day until God finally answered him at night, (Enos 1:4-5). God rewarded the brother of Jared because he prayed for a long time, (Ether 1:43). He gave the sons of Mosiah the expectation of suffering and affliction before they should expect success, (Alma 17:11), The sons of Mosiah show that they learned from God's intermittent reinforcement schedules when they split up for their missions with faith and hope that they will one day be reunited, (Alma 17:13). Nephi was rewarded with supernatural powers for his "unwearyingness" in declaring the word of God, (Hel 10:4-10). This introduces the hope that one could also be gifted with superpowers if they preach the word of God diligently enough. After the three days of darkness and natural disasters, the survivors were joyful and expressed thanksgiving to God when light returned, (3 Ne. 10:9-10). God promised the sons of Mosiah that if they endure suffering and afflictions, then God will make them instruments to bring more people to the faith, (Alma 17:11). All of these trials cause believers to expect that their needs and prayers will not be heeded immediately. This perspective strengthens their faith and hope, which prevents them from extinguishing their behaviors of reinforcing their beliefs and prayers. There is no set amount of prayer after which a person can discern that God is not answering.

God attempts to disguise this tactic as innocent while at the same time reinforcing its effectiveness by saying that His inactions or delays are to test the faith of His people. God tests the faith of His people in Helam by chastening them, but delivers them eventually, (Mosiah 23:21-24). God withheld information to test the faith of his people, (3 Ne. 26:11). By justifying His inaction and delay in this way, God influences His followers to sustain their hope when prayers seem ineffective because they think God could be testing their faith, and they are aware of the consequences they could be dealt for failing the test.

The Book of Mormon describes unlikely human behavior to provide evidence for reasoning in support of the faith. When Lehi prepared to take his family into the wilderness, his sons Laman and Lemuel wanted to stay in Jerusalem. They made a reasonable conclusion that their father was having hallucinations, and saw no benefit to leaving their property behind to risk their lives in the wilderness. They did not believe that they nor Jerusalem were in danger of destruction, but they obeyed their father and journeyed with him. Because of their murmuring in disagreement on the journey, their father, joined with the Holy Spirit, reprimanded them until they were shaking with fear, (1 Ne. 2:11-14). This is strange because Laman and Lemuel had already decided to concede to their father's order regardless of their opinions, yet the reprimand to ensure their obedience came after they set out on the journey. No fear of the power of the Holy Ghost or any other motive was explained before the journey began that would support Laman's and Lemuel's decisions to go with their father regardless of their strong opposition. Later, an angel appeared and spoke to Laman and Lemuel, yet they remained doubtful of the power of the Lord, (1 Ne. 3:29-31). After their third departure from Jerusalem, Laman and Lemuel, along with some of the family of Ishmael, protested against Nephi that they wanted to go back to Jerusalem, (1 Ne. 7:6-7). Nephi reminded his brothers of their vision of the angel to warn them that returning to Jerusalem would be a bad idea, (1 Ne. 7:10), but this only made the protesters angry. They restrained Nephi, intending to leave him in the wilderness to be eaten by wild animals, (1 Ne. 7:16). When Nephi escaped this and tried to speak to them again, they tried to restrain him again, but they decided not to when a couple people asked them not to kill Nephi. Then, the protesters asked Nephi for forgiveness, and they all continued toward the camp, (1 Ne. 7:18-21). If Laman and Lemuel truly did see the angel, it was very strange that they continued to disagree with the faith. There is no situational change described to explain why the protesters decided they wanted to return to Jerusalem after they had already chosen to depart Jerusalem with the group. Then, they decided that it was necessary to kill Nephi in order to have their way, instead of returning to Jerusalem without the faithful. After attempting to kill Nephi, they asked for forgiveness simply because a couple people asked them not to kill him, and then they continued on the journey with the faithful. This indicates that Laman and Lemuel changed their minds yet again, apparently with little to no influence.

Again, later on, Laman blamed Nephi for the sufferings of the journey, and declared to Lemuel and the sons of Ishmael that they should kill Nephi for causing their sufferings. He successfully entices them to join him in his anger, but the Lord's voice chastises them, and they repent for their defilement, (1 Ne. 16:20, 37-39). After God commanded Nephi to build a boat, Nephi's people murmured against him, expressing regret for making the journey out of Jerusalem, (1 Ne. 17:20-22). Nephi spoke to them in disagreement, and they responded with anger. They intended to drown Nephi, but Nephi warned them that He was armed with the power of God, so they receded, either due to their belief in Nephi's relationship with God, or due to possession by the Spirit of God, (1 Ne. 17:48, 52). While on the ocean, the people again become angry with Nephi for telling them to stop acting rude. Laman and Lemuel tied Nephi up with cords and treated him harshly, (1 Ne. 18:9-11). Eventually, because they feared sinking in a storm, they released Nephi and repented, (1 Ne. 18:20). After arriving in the promised land, Laman and Lemuel again tried to kill Nephi because they were jealous of him for having more power and leadership, (2 Ne. 5:2-3). All of this recurring aggressive rejection should not coincide with sustained membership with Nephi's tribe, nor is it consistent with their alleged fear of God's power shown to them before these aggressive incidents occurred.

Alma preached to a crowd of people described as "stiff-necked", (Alma 9:5). He began a speech by calling his audience wicked and perverse while they remained in control of their own rage and listened, (Alma 9:7-8). After listening to him speak for 22 more verses, the people permitted their anger against Alma and tried to grab him and throw him into prison, (Alma 9:32). It does not make sense to describe an offended crowd that listened and waited until Alma was done speaking before they took action against him as stiff-necked. This also happened with Abinadi when he was arrested under King Noah for his preaching and prophesying. He was first condemned to death in Mosiah 13:1, but he managed to delay his penalty because the priests became scared of his glowing face, (Mosiah 13:5). Abinadi took the opportunity to evangelize to the priests for the next 86 verses, after which the king again commanded that he be put to death, (Mosiah 17:1). By waiting 86 verses for Abinadi to finish his sermon, it seems that the authorities simply decided not to assert their power over Abinadi anymore since he had scared them with a miraculous glow. When he was still condemned after he finished talking, we can interpret that the authorities were not afraid to condemn him to death. Their fear was suddenly irrelevant. If fear is not the explanation for why the authorities waited for Abinadi to finish his sermon before taking action again, no other reason for the wait is apparent. The church conveniently benefits with scripture of completed, uninterrupted sermons.

Alma, who witnessed these occurrences, begged the king to release Abinadi, but the king had Alma cast out, and then sent his servants after him to kill him. Alma fled and hid before he was caught, (Mosiah 17:2-4) If begging that someone condemned to death be spared warrants a death sentence, it does not make sense that Alma was cast out, and then immediately chased down to be brought back.

After three days in prison, Abinadi was brought to the king again. Again, Abinadi threatened the king with the power of God, and the king hesitated to release him out of fear. The priests quickly convinced the king to anger against Abinadi again, and the king authorized Abinadi's death penalty. Abinadi was scourged and burned to death, (Mosiah 17:11-14). Here we can see that the king changed his state of mind two additional times, and the priests who were once fearful of Abinadi for his miraculous glow, seem to have forgotten the miracle and their fear of God. Rapid attitude change like this is not normal. Witnessing the supernatural power of God is a strong reason for a person to change their mind, and an abnormal experience like a miracle should be difficult to forget about. Personal experience has been shown to be a positive factor in the strength of an attitude in comparison to attitudes that are not supported by personal experience, (Regan and Fazio, 1977). This fear was especially strong because the king and priests were already firm in their anger against Abinadi, yet their personal experience allowed their fear to become even greater than their anger. The priests' fear of God became dominant over their opinions that Abinadi should be killed, and this new attitude should have been practically impossible to change in that short amount of time because of its strength. Regardless, the fearful attitude was overcome by the time the priests encouraged the king to redeclare his death sentence for Abinadi. Any anger the priests had in the three days between the time of the miracle and the final death sentence should not have been enough to override their established fear of a supernaturally powerful enemy.

Ammon, a Nephite, and King Lamoni journeyed to rescue Ammon's brothers from prison. While on their journey, they crossed paths with Lamoni's father. Lamoni's father was angry with his son for befriending a Nephite, so he commanded his son to kill Ammon. When Lamoni refused, his father attempted to slay his own son, but Ammon prevented the killing, (Alma 20:14-17). Lamoni argued that his reason for attempting to kill his son was because if he did, it would be Ammon's fault, (Alma 20:19). When Lamoni's father feared that Ammon could kill him, he agreed to release Ammon's brothers from prison. When Lamoni's father perceived that Ammon had no desire to kill him, he was impressed, and expressed honor and desire to get to know Ammon better, (Alma 20:26-27). Even though it is explained, Lamoni's father immediately overcame his prejudice against Ammon, which is unusual behavior. Humans rarely change their views immediately like this, even when new or different information is provided, (Anderson, Lepper and Ross, 1980). This rapid change of mind indicates that Lamoni's father had simply chosen to be evil without any sufficient reason.

After a speech from their king, the Anti-Nephi-Lehis decided to bury their swords, and never use weapons for the shedding of blood again, (Alma 24:17-18). When the Lamanites battled against them, the Anti-Nephi-Lehis prostrated before them, and the Lamanites slayed 1005 of them. Immediately after this battle, the

Lamanites repented, (Alma 24:21-24). This is not the most likely outcome because before going into battle, each Lamanite made their own non-rushed individual decision to comply with the attack on the Anti-Nephi-Lehis. Good or bad, they already had their reasons for battle, so they likely would have sustained those reasons after the battle, and could have used those reasons as protection against uncomfortable feelings of shame if they needed to. Instead, we have a story of an army which killed people meaninglessly as if they were nonintellectual animals.

Alma rejected the offer to become king because he believed that the role would cause people to give him a greater, unequal value compared to those of other citizens, (Mosiah 23:6-7). Contrary to his perspective, Alma accepted a different role that could have the same effect: the position of high priest, (Mosiah 23:16). This is strange because human cognition and behavior naturally gravitate toward consistency, (Heider, 1946).

Because of the fall of Adam, humans are devilish by nature, (Alma 42:9-10). Those who remain in their fallen nature are subject to the power of the devil, (Mosiah 16:3-5). Unbelievers are depicted as naturally bad people, regardless of whether or not these depictions are probable. The testament has a motive for demonstrating this because of its assertion that nothing that is good denies Christ, but acknowledges that He is, (Moro. 10:6). Alternative beliefs happen because of evil disposition. Just three years after the miraculous sign of Jesus Christ's birth which was a night that remained as bright as daylight, many people began to disbelieve. They theorized that the sign was wrought by people and the devil working together to draw people away from God. The scripture explains that these unbelievers were deceived by the devil because of their vanity, (3 Ne. 2:2). Evil behavior or abstinence of virtue is commensurate with denial against the faith. To provide evidence that denial of faith is evil, it is associated with crime. Nephites were denied the strength of God and subsequently slaughtered because of their riches, withholding help from the needy, smiting humble brethren on the cheek, mocking sacred things, denying the spirit of prophecy and revelation, murdering, plundering, lying, stealing, adultery, and rising up in great contentions, and asking the Lamanites to fight Nephites, (Hel. 4:11-13). Those who believe that children should be baptized do not have charity, (Moro. 8:14). The curse of dark skin for unbelief directly caused people to be idle, and full of mischief and subtlety, (2 Ne. 5:21-24). Some people desire to do evil as its own benefit, (Alma 42:28).

This contention that people are inherently evil is not accurate. People strive to maintain their self concepts of being morally directed, (Harmon-Jones and Mills, 1999). When people commit immoral acts, they disengage from morality with rationalizations in order to protect themselves from the discomfort of knowing that they acted immorally, (Bandura, 2016). People do not want to be evil. People tend to think of themselves as kinder than most people, (Epley and Dunning, 2000). Preverbal babies have a preference for characters who exhibit helping behavior over characters who exhibit hindering behavior, (Hamlin, Wynn and Bloom, 2007). Toddlers perform helping behaviors without being prompted, (Warneken, 2013). The testament provides plenty of examples of characters who are evil at heart, including those who desired to destroy the believers in 3 Ne. 1:16, and judges who made covenants together against righteousness, (3 Ne. 6:27-30). There was even a church established that persecuted the church of Christ for the reason that His church taught people to be humble, preached the faith of Christ, and was blessed with miracles, (4 Ne. 1:29). Similarly, in 1 Ne. 13:5-9, an evil church is prophesied to kill and torture saints for the praise of their audience. Speaking to a multitude in the city of Ammonihah, Amulek accused the multitude of setting traps against God's followers and plotting to bring destruction on God's people, (Alma 10:17-18). Unbelievers who actually did believe in the church of Christ decisively rebelled against it, (3 Ne. 6:18; 4 Ne. 1:38).

Lehi described a dream he had. In the dream, he found a fruit tree, and he tasted the fruit. The fruit filled his soul with joy, and he described it as the best fruit, (1 Ne. 8:12). The tree is called the tree of life, and represents the love of God, (1 Ne. 11:25). He described a river leading to the tree, and an iron rod that aligned with the bank of the river. On the other side of the river was a great and spacious building where people were enjoying materials of quality. The building represented the pride of the world, (1 Ne. 11:36). The people in the building were focused on mocking those who were seeking and enjoying the fruit, (1 Ne. 8:27). This dream presents unlikely behavior of those who were in the building. Non-believers do not typically focus their attention and motivations on mocking believers. People are focused on themselves as the main characters of their own lives. Non-believers are not immersed in the pleasure and pride of the world for the purpose of successful competition against the believers for happiness. They are focused on their own interpretations of their environments and their own desires. In a similar vision Lehi's son Nephi had, nations of people gathered together to fight against the followers of Christ, (1 Ne. 11:34-36).

Laban refused to surrender his property to the sons of Lehi, which created an obstacle against God's plan. He saw the sons of Lehi as robbers and forced them off his land. This was understandable until Laban sent his servants after the sons of Lehi to kill them and steal their belongings, (1 Ne. 3:25). Because he created an obstacle to God's plan, Laban fits into the category of evil people. Laban's evil behavior of stealing was provided as a means to confirm the church's negative judgment of him as correct.

After Laman and Lemuel saw an angel, (1 Ne. 3:29-31), they remained in doubt, providing an example of unbelievers who chose unbelief because of unfounded evil intent. The reoccurring attempts to kill Nephi discussed earlier also demonstrate the evil of unbelievers, as eliminating Nephi would have been unnecessary for those unbelievers to attain what they wanted.

A lawyer named Zeezrom desired to destroy goodness, (Alma 11:21). He challenged Amulek on the teachings of God. By the end of Amulek's response, Zeezrom was trembling, (Alma 11:46). This indicated that he believed Amulek's teachings, because Amulek spoke of the danger of abiding in Hell for evil behavior, (Alma 11:37), and Zeezrom felt guilty in response, (Alma 12:1). He continued becoming more scared as Alma continued to speak to him, (Alma 12:7, 14:6). Zeezrom knew that he was challenging what he believed, and he felt guilty and in danger of Hell, yet he desired to destroy goodness. Next to nobody desires to be someone that destroys goodness. Zeezrom was soon baptized and immediately began preaching, (Alma 15:12). He quickly transitioned out of his state of guilt and shame. If Zeezrom truly hated the faith, his rapid change of attitude was not normal, (Anderson, Lepper and Ross, 1980).

Korihor, the atheist who was struck dumb for expressing his requirement of a sign from God in order to have faith in Christ, admitted that he lied about his unbelief. He wrote that he was visited by the devil who told him to teach people that God does not exist, and that he began to believe the devil, (Alma 30:52-53). Korihor's unquestioning obedience of this devil was not associated nor implied with any motive. Also, even though he received these instructions from an angel, he still began to believe that there is no god. Similarly, Sherem preached against Christ, but he later professed faith in God and admitted that he was deceived by the devil to speak against God, (Jacob 7:1-2, 17-18).

Even though they are not realistic, if they are believed, these psychological inaccuracies would provide support for the claim that either a person is a righteous member of the right church, or they are a member of the church of abomination, (1 Ne. 14:10). God separates mankind into two categories: His people, and the wicked, (2 Ne. 23:22), therefore there is a motive to convey this throughout the Book of Mormon. In Alma 46:1, all the people who did not follow Helaman's preachings joined together against him. Divided opinion, neutrality, uncertainty, and disinterest were not chosen by anyone.

To manipulate means to coax a person's emotions to override their logical thinking, with the goal of changing the person's behavior for a benefit that is not for the victim, while disregarding the respect due to that person. Manipulation is a misuse of faith. Emotions that are coaxed out of followers of the Book of Mormon such as guilt for the bloodshed of Christ, the fear of Hell, and longing to be loved or honored as a holy saint, are all coaxed to become more important to the person than the honest search for truth. The Book of Mormon claims that its purpose is to benefit the followers, but as we examined earlier, God's perfect behavior not only failed to always provide people with what was best for them, but His true profile seems to be a harmful one against mankind. Understanding the proper use of faith, we can apply it to common scientific and historical doubts from the Book of Mormon to help determine if it could be offering sincere salvation to us under the immense power and full knowledge of God, or if it disregards truth, alluding to a hidden motive.

Chapter 3

The Truth

Possibly the easiest way to determine if a testament is reliable is to examine it for conflicts with what we know about science and history. The following conflicts might feel irrelevant to the believer since the scripture is already upheld as truth, and it is unnecessary to resolve these conflicts for salvation, but regardless, it is still important for the believer to be aware of the frequency of these conflicts, and their prominence in comparison to reality, especially from an external perspective, as these truths should pave the way for strong faith. These are the truths of the scriptures that God preserved for the purpose of leading the unbelievers to put faith in the church and to bring them to salvation, making these conflicts a much more serious issue for the unbeliever than for the believer. This chapter will only scratch the surface for the most obvious conflicts, being most useful to those who are less familiar with the Book of Mormon, but there is other, more scholarly literature out there that focus entirely on topics like these, both offensively and defensively. If science and history agree with the reasoning behind the commandments of the church, then discrepancies of God's character and the church's improper use of faith could be irrelevant against them.

Consistent with the teachings of most Christian churches, the Book of Mormon claims that the mother of The Messiah was a virgin beyond motherhood. Nephi, son of Lehi, received a prophetic vision that confirmed the virginity of the mother of the Son of God. An angel said to Nephi, "Behold, the virgin whom thou seest is the mother of the Son of God, after the manner of the flesh", (1 Ne. 11:18). Alma prophesied of Mary, a virgin, who conceives a son by the power of the Holy Ghost, (Alma 7:10). A miracle by definition is a contradiction against science, and in the form of testimony, it requires an immensely greater amount of faith than a testimony of a natural occurrence would.

The Book of Mormon contradicts science regarding skin color. God cursed Lamanite unbelievers with a dark skin as a punishment for their iniquities:

And he had caused the cursing to come upon them, yea, even a sore cursing, because of their iniquity. For behold, they had hardened their hearts against him, that they had become like unto a flint; wherefore, as they were white, and exceedingly fair and delightsome, that they might not be enticing unto my people the Lord God did cause a skin of blackness to come upon them. (2 Ne. 5:21)

The dark skin itself is described as a curse, and it is inherited by anyone born of these Lamanites. None of these verses make any indication that this skin color

66

change occurred gradually through lineage or mutation. On the contrary, the curse of the Amilicites, a tribe of Lamanites, confirms that skin color changes like this happened instantly. The Amilicites unknowingly activated the curse of a skin color when they colored their foreheads red, (Alma 3:18). The curse of the dark skin was eventually lifted from the Lamanites and they became white like the Nephites and were united with the Nephite civilization, (3 Ne. 2:14-16). Instant skin color changes like these are miracles. Although these changes in skin color are called curses, the explanation for describing skin color change in this way is less than weak. Complimenting this, lighter skin color is a sign of righteousness. Abinadi's skin color glowed as he preached to the priests of King Noah, (Mosiah 13:5). The disciples of Jesus in the New World "did pray steadfastly, without ceasing, unto him; and he did smile upon them again; and behold they were white, even as Jesus", (3 Ne. 19:30). Jacob 3:8 confirms that darker skin color is caused by sin. The curse of dark skin was described as a curse because it caused certain behaviors including idleness, mischief, and subtlety, (2 Ne. 5:21, 24), and also because the color distinguishes these people from the Nephites to discourage the Nephites from breeding with them, (Alma 3:14). If skin color caused these behavioral effects as the testament claims, then that causation is a miracle. As for the curse being that the Lamanites are distinguished from the Nephites, this does not support that the skin color itself is the curse, but that the curse is the discrimination against them. In reality, skin color is not to blame for discrimination. Discriminators and culture are to blame for discrimination. Skin color is not a curse of itself.

Reading someone else's thoughts would be a miracle. This happened once at Alma 10:17, and another time at Alma 18:16. Sure one could argue that these statements are not literally telling us that people are reading other's thoughts, but literal interpretation is always valid, and usually preferred from a fair and objective perspective. Another cognitive miracle is described in Ether 3:22 where God declares that Jared's brother will be able to write in a language that nobody can interpret.

A miraculous earthquake occurs in Alma 14. Two prophets, Alma and Amulek, are imprisoned for their preaching in the city of Ammonihah. While bound in prison, they are struck by the chief judge, and some priests, lawyers, and teachers. Alma cried out to the Lord for deliverance, (Alma 14:26). An earthquake occurs, collapsing the prison walls and killing the chief judge, priests, lawyers, and teachers who struck Alma and Amulek. Alma and Amulek survive the earthquake unharmed, and their survival is attributed to the power of their faith in Christ, (Alma 14:27-28). The earthquake was caused by Alma's prayer, and the people there were selected to survive or die according to their faith in Christ. Following the earthquake, people of the city of Ammonihah flocked to the prison to understand what caused the loud noises, (Alma 14:29). No earthquake is so centralized that it can topple walls of a prison causing such noise that multitudes of people in the same city flock to see what happened, while also not having felt the earthquake elsewhere in the city. A true earthquake this powerful would not leave other city dwellers unknowing of it, nor leave them focused on the noise coming from the collapse of a single building.

Some miracles are related to movement. The testament describes a time when a prophet named Nephi was protected from people who tried to grab him to take him to prison. God took Nephi, and Nephi was "conveyed away out of the midst of them", (Hel. 10:16). This portrays God as intervening in a scenario which would have otherwise left Nephi vulnerable to the people. There is nothing scientific about travel described in this way. Another transportation miracle occurred when Jesus Christ arrived in Bountiful among the Nephites. Jesus descended from heaven, (3 Ne. 11:8). To prove that his physical body descended from heaven, Jesus had the people thrust their hands into his side and feel his wounds, (3 Nephi 11:15). Jesus ascended back into heaven in 3 Nephi 18:39. Another movement miracle was a curse of disappearing tools described in Ether 14:1.

There were cosmic miracles too. To fulfill a prophecy as a sign of the birth of the Son of God, the sky did not get dark after sunset, (3 Ne. 1:15). In 3 Nephi 8:21-23, there is darkness in the land that lasts for the time of three days. During this time, it is impossible to create light, and nothing gives light from the sky. There is also a prophecy that one day, the earth will be wrapped together as a scroll, (3 Ne. 26:3; Morm. 5:23, 9:2). Gravitational pull would not allow this to happen. The earth is spherical because gravity pulls all of the earth towards it's center. It would take an impossible combination of forces to cause the spherical earth to become like a rolled-up scroll, even for just a passing moment. Earth could be destroyed by a cosmic collision, or it could be absorbed into the Sun after the Sun becomes a red giant, but science does not recognize any prediction or possibility of the world ending by becoming flattened out enough to be reasonably compared to a scroll, and then rolling together. If this is a metaphor, it is a dangerous one for the plausibility of the Book of Mormon, because of the other miracles the scripture declares, and because it is written as a prophecy.

Instant healing of sickness occurs in Alma 15:5-11. A convert to the faith, Zeezrom, is sick in bed and has a fever. When Alma cries unto the Lord to heal Zeezrom according to Zeezrom's faith, Zeezrom heals instantly and leaps up onto his feet and walks. The disciple Nephi raised his brother from the dead after he had been stoned to death, (3 Ne. 7:19). The chosen disciples of Jesus performed miracles including healing the sick, raising the dead, causing the lame to walk, giving sight to the blind, and giving hearing to the deaf, (4 Ne. 1:5).

The prophet Ammon taught King Lamoni about the church and the prophecy of redemption for sin. Afterward, King Lamoni cried out to the Lord for mercy and fell to the ground as if dead, and remained like this for two days. His condition was so dead-like that his family mourned over him, convinced that he was dead. They even laid his body in a sepulcher, (Alma 18:42-43, 19:1). He came back to life miraculously on the day that Ammon prophesied that he would, (Alma 19:11-12). After experiencing the joy of returning to consciousness on earth, King Lamoni again sank down to the ground, followed by the queen, then Ammon, and then servants to the king. The falling is caused by being overpowered by joy, the Spirit, gratitude, and calling out to the Lord, (Alma 19:13-16). Just one chapter later, as another miracle of the same type, the father of king Lamoni prayed for a sign, and was "struck as if he were dead", and the prophet Aaron raised him back up to his strength, (Alma 22:18, 22).

Jesus's chosen disciples were thrown into prisons that could not hold them, thrown into pits in the ground only to be rescued by God, and they were cast into furnaces and remained unharmed, (3 Ne. 28:19-21). Members of the church were miraculously protected from burning, (4 Ne. 1:32). In Alma 57:25-26, Helaman stated that of his 2060 men at the battle, not a single man was killed in the battle, and 1000 of the Lamanite army had been slain. Helaman describes these results as miraculous, and attributes this success to the power of God because of the faith of his army.

A topographic miracle occurred in 3 Nephi 8:10 when a storm caused the entire city of Moronihah to become a mountain.

The Book of Mormon consistently describes incidences of the voice of God being heard by many people at once. A claim like this cannot even be explained neurologically, since more than a single person heard the same miraculous voice. In an incident when contention arose within Nephi's tribe to kill Nephi, God chastens these people:

And it came to pass that the Lord was with us, yea, even the voice of the Lord came and did speak many words unto them, and did chasten them exceedingly; and after they were chastened by the voice of the Lord they did turn away their anger, and did repent of their sins, insomuch that the Lord did bless us again with food, that we did not perish. (1 Ne. 16:39)

In another incident, the voice of God comes to some Lamanites from a cloud over prophets Nephi and Lehi,

(Hel. 5:29, 32-33). In this setting, Nephi and Lehi, sons of Helaman, are prisoners of the Lamanites, and Nephi and Lehi appear to be within fire but are not being burned. The prophets tell the Lamanites that God is showing them this fire, and an earthquake immediately follows, (Hel. 5:23-27). These occurrences are witnessed by 300 people who saw angels, and declared what they saw to others, (Hel. 5:48-50).

After Jesus's death, God caused natural disasters in the promised land of the Book of Mormon, and following the disasters, the voice of God is heard by everyone on the land. He takes responsibility for the destruction, including the unrealistic sinking of Moroni city, and the covering of the city called Moronihah, (3 Ne. 9:1-22). Just before Jesus Christ arrives in the New World, a voice is heard from heaven by a multitude, (3 Ne. 11:1, 11:3-5). The voice says, "Behold my Beloved Son, in whom I am well pleased, in whom I have glorified my name-hear ye him", (3 Ne. 11:6-7), attributing this voice to God.

As impossible as miracles are, for most of them, we cannot use history to verify whether or not they happened. However, there are several things mentioned in the Book of Mormon that do conflict with our knowledge of history. Note that according to 1 Nephi 10:4, the followers of Lehi who left Jerusalem for the promised land departed around the year 600 BC. They became disconnected from advancements and discoveries from that part of the world occurring after that time. The Jaredites of the book of Ether came to the Americas from across the Atlantic after the time of the confounding of languages at the Tower of Babel, (Ether 1:33), at approximately 2,200 BC. Human DNA tells a different story. According to genetic research, all indigenous peoples of the Americas descended from Siberian populations by crossing to the North American continent through Beringia between 20,000 and 15,000 years before present, (BP), before Beringia became submerged under the ocean, (Schurr and Sherry, 2004).

On their journey toward the promised land of the New World, God asked Lehi, perhaps in a dream, to take his tribe on a journey into the wilderness, (1 Ne. 16:9). The following morning, Lehi found a compass outside his tent. The compass was meant to guide them through the wilderness. A spindle on the compass pointed in the direction they were to travel, (1 Ne. 16:10). The tribe journeys in a south-south-east direction, (1 Ne. 16:13), indicating that the compass did not simply point north. Compasses were not known outside of China until the time of Medieval Europe. Lehi's compass contained writing that changed based on the faith of the people, (1 Ne. 16:29). Everything about the compass Lehi found was miraculous.

Iron and steel are mentioned several times in this testament. In the New World, Nephi taught his tribe to work with metals which included iron and steel, (2 Ne. 5:15). In the book of Jarom, the Nephites become rich in materials including iron and steel, (Jarom 8). The people of Lib also mined for and worked with iron, (Ether 10:23). There is no evidence to support the claim that indigenous peoples in the Americas were processing iron or steel before the Europeans arrived. Pure iron cannot simply be mined because it oxidizes. Iron oxides need to be smelted to be consolidated into a useful form. Steel is an iron alloy. Its production involves the additional process of adjusting the carbon content of iron so that it is more sturdy than wrought iron, but more flexible than cast iron, which requires a temperature high enough to melt iron, and techniques for controlling its carbon content.

Zeniff's tribe farmed wheat, barley, neas, and sheum, (Mosiah 9:9). Wheat and barley were not present in the Americas until after the arrival of the Spaniards. *Hordeum vulgare* is the name of the domesticated species of barley we still farm today which has been cultivated since the civilization of ancient Mesopotamia. This is different from *Hordeum pusillum*, a wild species of *Hordeum* found growing in the Americas. *Hordeum pusillum* and *Hordeum vulgare* do not share a common ancestor until over nine million years ago, with both lineages diverging multiple times since then, placing *Hordeum pusillum* far outside of the gene pool for breeding with *Hordeum vulgare* for fertile offspring, (Stein and Muehlbauer, 2018). It is possible that *Hordeum pusillum*, commonly known as "little barley", may have been domesticated in the ancient Americas. However, the seeds of this plant were still much smaller than those of barley, so without large crops and technology to increase efficiency, it would have been an inefficient source of nourishment. Evidence of large crops of little barley from the pre-Columbian Americas have yet to be found. There is little to nothing to support that neas and sheum existed. These two words for types of grain were first introduced in the English translation of the Book of Mormon. Because of this, the argument that the word "wheat" in this scripture refers to another type of grain that was present in the pre-Columbian Americas does not work, because like neas and sheum, an alternative word would have been translated for whatever grain these peoples were calling "wheat" as well.

Among many of the weapons mentioned in this testament are cimeters. Cimeters describe a specific type of blade which is curved. Indigenous peoples of the Americas did not have cimeters. Wooden clubs and macuahuitls, which they did have, do not accurately translate in English as cimeters. Regardless, several tribes mentioned in this book have had cimeters. Zeniff's tribe, (Mosiah 9:16), the Nephite army led by Moroni, (Alma 43:18), the army of Zerahemnah, (Alma 43:20), and the Lamanites in Helaman 1:14, all had cimeters. Moroni also mentions cimeters in Alma 60:2.

Another item that peoples in the Americas of Book of Mormon should not have had was linen. Linen is mentioned in Alma 1:29; 4:6, Helaman 6:13, Ether 9:17, and Ether 10:24. Linen is a textile made from the flax plant. Flax was not present in the precolumbian Americas. To say that by "linen" the testament was referring to a different type of textile is a frail defense because the Book of Mormon regularly mentions "clothing", (1 Ne. 13:7, 8; 2 Ne. 13:6, 7; 28:13; Mosiah 10:5; Alma 1:29; 14:22; 43:19; Hel. 4:12; 6:13). If the "linen" was not actually linen, it should have been translated either as a new English word, as "clothing" or "cloth", or it should have been translated descriptively as cloth made from a specified plant.

Horses are consistently present in the Americas of the Book of Mormon, and were found there, living in the wilderness, (1 Ne. 18:25; Alma 18:10-12, 20:6; 3 Ne. 3:22, 21:14; Ether 9:19). Some of these verses also mentioned chariots, and Ether 9:19 also mentioned other animals useful to the people which were elephants, and cureloms and cumoms. Prior to the European invasion of the New World, wheels were not used there for practical uses such as for chariots. Horses were extinct in the Americas by 2,200 BC and did not return until after the Europeans arrived. A generous estimate dates the youngest pre-Columbian horse specimen found among the Americas to be no more recent than 7,600 years BP, (Haile et al., 2009), which calculates to 5,650 BC. The youngest ancient horse specimens of South America are no more recent than 6,050 BC, (Alberdi and Prado, 1993; Prado, Sànchez and Alberdi, 2011). Elephant-like animals in the Americas were also extinct long before 2,200 BC. The youngest evidence of gomphotheres in North America dates to as recently as 11,545 BC, (Sanchez et al., 2014), and the extinction of the gomphothere in South America is placed late in the Pleistocene Epoch, (Avilla et al., 2013). Excluding remains from disconnected and therefore irrelevant islands, the most recent mammoth remains of the Americas are not more recent than 8,550 BC, (Haile et al., 2009). The youngest specimen of mastodon is dated to be as generously recent as 8,042 BC. However, by accuracy rather than generosity, gomphotheres, mammoths, and mastodons were extinct before 8,050 BC, (Meltzer and Mead, 1983). If we include the evidence of mammoths that survived on islands, the youngest specimen of mammoth found was calculated to have died at around 2,050 BC, but this evidence is irrelevant for the Book of Mormon because Wrangel island became an island about 5000 years earlier than that, (Vartanyan et. al., 2008). The age of the mammoth remains found on St. Paul Island in the Pribilofs of Alaska are approximated to 3,750 BC, (Veltre et al., 2008), still before the Jaradites of the book of Ether arrived on the other side of the land mass only neighboring the island. There no evidence that elephants ever lived in the ancient Americas, and there

76

is nothing to support the existence of cureloms and cumoms outside of the Book of Mormon. Cureloms and cumoms hinder the claims of the testament further, because even if it were argued that the terms "horse" or "elephant" in the Book of Mormon actually refer to different but comparable animals with no English equivalent words to describe them at the time that the book was translated, the terms "cureloms" and "cumoms" were used to label other animals that the Jews would not have had words for. Therefore, the elephant or horse-like animals would have been given their own names as well. Also, the Nephites were not referring to deer when they spoke of horses because the Nephites originated out of Jerusalem where they would have known of the antelope, an animal which was more comparable to deer of the New World than horses were. Roes are mentioned in the Bible in association with Jerusalem, (Song 2:7, 9, 17). If the bible books written on the brass plates from Laban included this book, it would be even stranger for these peoples to have labeled deer as horses.

According to Alma 7:10, the Son of God was prophesied to be born in Jerusalem, which conflicts with the Bible which states that the Son of God was born in Bethlehem, (Matt. 2:1; Luke 2:4-7).

Language history does not agree with the book of Mormon. Alma lectured his son Corianton for "going after" a harlot named Isabel, (Alma 39:3). The name Isabel is a Spanish form of the name Elizabeth from the middle ages, (Hanks, Hardcastle and Hodges, 2007). The Spanish language was not developed before the Nephites left Jerusalem, and it originated from the Iberian Peninsula on the opposite side of the Mediterranean Sea. It is easy to say that it could have been a coincidence that the name Isabel was used by a civilization with no connection to the Spanish language, but until the ancient usage of the name Isabel is found elsewhere, or until its origins are supported with linguistic history prior to, or not connected to the development of Old Castilian, that theory is not supported against history. Also, the languages the Nephites could have known from ancient Jerusalem do not include Reformed Egyptian. According to Moroni, the plates of record were written in Reformed Egyptian, (Morm. 9:32-33). Outside the Book of Mormon, there is no evidence that this language ever existed.

Although He is a god of miracles, the scriptures tell us that God is unchanging, (Morm. 9:19). God's unchanging nature of the universe reflects His perfect plan, like a software that was created with flawless non-improvable coding that therefore should not be modified. God is all-knowing, so with nothing to learn, He does not change. He already knows the best way. When God allows a miracle, He changes, because miracles break the laws of nature which He created in the beginning to sustain any variations of the presentation of the universe He deemed perfect for us. So, a God of miracles is actually a changing God. The scientific and historical truths declared in the Book of Mormon do not rise above doubts regarding the character of God or of faith, but instead, contribute to those doubts. However, if the Book of Mormon provides effective guidance for spiritual health, perhaps none of these doubts will be able to threaten the faith against that benefit.

Chapter 4

The Life

Many people believe that truth is not the most important focus for seeking spiritual health, and there is a fair argument for that. This is the engineer's perspective. An engineer seeks methods that produce the results they want. Unlike scientists, they are less interested in knowing the science and math of why methods work. They are mainly interested in getting good results. The engineer's perspective is not inferior or in opposition to that of scientists. Engineering can create new knowledge and questions for scientists to explore. Like engineers, many believers in the Book of Mormon are primarily seeking good spiritual health, and the inaccuracies of the book are not relevant to them. This chapter seeks to expose imperfections in the Book of Mormon as a guide for spiritual health. If no imperfections can be found to justify a verdict against the testament's spiritual value, the following prosecutions against it can be dismissed.

The Book of Mormon is structured to produce Stockholm syndrome. Stockholm syndrome is the phenomenon of a victim bonding or sympathizing with their abusive captor. The formulation of Stockholm syndrome begins when the victim perceives that they cannot escape from the abuser, or that their escape is not worth the consequences. Immersed in these circumstances, the victim learns that they have to accept their position. When they do this, victims of the syndrome rationalize that they prefer to be submissive to the abuser, or that they cannot do better, or do not deserve better. This could be because they do not want to believe that they failed or made a mistake, especially if they rejected a way out of the situation.

To maintain control, the captor distances the victim from all escape outlets. This could involve taking power away from the victim, isolating the victim, or chastising escape options. Depending on the situation, escape outlets could be the ability to scream for help, access to doors or windows, or they could be ideas, information, social groups, confidence, or friends that could influence the victim to leave the abuser.

The victim's most preferred escape outlet becomes the captor themself. If the victim can escape the abuse with permission from the abuser, or otherwise knowing that the abuser is no longer a threat, it would be the most safe and comfortable escape for them. Not only does this fortify the victim's compliance, but it could also cause the victim to further rationalize or come to believe that their decision to comply is something they prefer to do freely. Stockholm syndrome requires the abuser to grant minimal hope or benefit for the victim in order to sustain their preference for that bond and mental submission. This is especially important in the beginning of the relationship before the attachment is formed. Without any benefits or hope, the victim is likely to reconsider their submission, seeking to learn about any way out of the relationship.

The victim has a high interest in understanding the abuser because the abuser determines vital outcomes in their life. This could be regarding things like health, life direction, life-altering decisions, mood, hope, and power. Having been distanced from other opportunities of power and sources of influence, the victim needs to be in favor of the captor in order to retain their own resilience. With this high interest, the victim tries to understand the mind of the abuser so they can understand what influence they have on the abuser, and thus vicariously control their own life. This effort to understand the abuser causes the victim to sympathize or bond with the abuser's perspective. This sympathy further fortifies the victim's loyalty to the abuser.

With this loyalty and reduced and condensed access to power, the victim may begin to anticipate the abuser's desires and demands, and enforce them onto themself and onto opposing influence, on behalf of the abuser. They do this to stay safely in favor of the abuser, but they also do this to protect their escape outlets. The thought process here is that if the victim can enforce their own distance from outlets, they can at least keep them on the horizon if they decide to use them someday, instead of allowing or making use of them, which would make the outlets vulnerable to harsher restriction or elimination by the abuser.

Learned helplessness is also a factor in Stockholm syndrome. By accepting their position as victim, the victim has spared themselves the continued anguish of exhausted hope of escape. However, learned helplessness also preserves the victim in a normality that would forget that reconsideration of hope is an option. Because of learned helplessness, the victim might remain submissive to the abuser even after the abuser loses power, or when escape options increase in reliability or decrease in consequence.

Having this understanding of the formulation of Stockholm syndrome, we can expose how it is being solicited by the Book of Mormon. Once a person is made aware of the teachings of the church, they are threatened with eternal damnation if they do not follow its laws. Even those who hesitate to believe in the claims of the scripture may sway to choose to submit to the authority of the church because they decipher that the chance of eternal Hell is too great of a risk against compliance. Once a person installs the faith of the church within themselves, the safest and most comfortable escape route from the invasive control on their life is compliance until natural death. People often or usually develop this faith because they seek love and attachment with those who promote it to them. Followers persist in their faith because they are given hope for a relationship with God and freedom in the afterlife.

By teaching and testifying of the unproven reward of eternal happiness and of other rewards for faith demonstrated within the scriptures including prosperity, supernatural powers, and answered prayers, believers are inveigled to hope for the same from their unchanging God. Among the beliefs the church forces onto its followers is the belief that God is good. However, God has violated morality. God commanded the sons of Lehi to steal without the purpose of immediate survival, (1 Ne. 3:4), and to kill a man who was so drunk that he couldn't stand, (1 Ne. 4:7, 12). He used us for our sins, (2 Ne. 2:24-25; 10:3). He endorsed nations to have war against the unbelieving Jews through generations until the Jews believe in Christ, (2 Ne. 25:15-16). He provoked prejudice based on skin color, (Alma 3:6-9). If doubts against the good character of God are sustainable, then He is not trustworthy, and His misleading good reputation becomes part of the recipe for Stockholm syndrome. Love does not require trust. A good parent loves their child deeply but does not necessarily trust them in many things. The faith of the Book of Mormon fuses trust and love such that to love God without faith in Him to know and do what is best for us, or to love God without trusting the church, is considered invalid or even impossible. The enforcement of faith is beneficial to the Church for controlling and isolating its members. Together, God's good reputation and the rewards for having faith are enough for the church to provide victims with the substantial benefit needed to preserve their preference to stay with the church and mentally submit to its desires and commands.

To limit the communal powers of its followers, the scripture feeds its victims with chastisement of affiliation with wealth. Wealth is assumed to directly cause evil, (2 Ne. 9:30; Alma 4:6-8; 3 Ne. 6:15). It is categorized among evil behaviors such as assault, murder, and stealing, (Hel. 4:11-13, 7:21-22), in the effort that the believer will adapt the assumption that having wealth is evil of itself. God despises those who are rich, (2 Ne. 9:42), punishes them, (Hel. 4:11-13, 7:21-22), and condemns them to Hell, (2 Ne. 28:15).

Wealth is not equivalent to evil. Many people, when given means for power, will exploit it, but it is not evil simply to have wealth. Wealth is condemned by the scripture because the church knows that it gives people a way to gain power and satisfaction. The church wants its victims to depend on it for those things. A prophet named Alma was happy to find that there were poor people who were not allowed to enter the synagogues and were humbled in their afflictions, because he knew that these people would be more open to his teachings, (Alma 32:4-6). These people were perfect targets for the church because they are more likely to have envy for the wealthy than people who are not poor, so a church that validates their envy and provides them with a way to feel more righteous than the rich is appealing to them. Having encouraged the faithful to avoid wealth, wealth is then used as bait to influence believers into placing hope in Christ, (Jacob 2:19). Although the wealth mentioned in these verses is only given to those with intent to perform acts of charity, this is enough to show from scripture that wealth is not evil. The church is more successful at influencing people when its victims are in want or need.

The church goes directly to the source of their victim's power by intimately invading the spirit. This is done by stealing thought and responsibility. The church condemns objective investigation of its claims by its improper use of faith. By requiring faith before knowledge, the faithful are made to dismiss all of their own contradicting thoughts. The scripture speaks of Korihor the anti-Christ who preached the following perspective on responsibility:

And many more such things did he say unto them, telling them that there could be no atonement made for the sins of men, but every man fared in this life according to the management of the creature; therefore every man prospered according to his genius, and that every man conquered according to his strength; and whatsoever a man did was no crime.

And thus he did preach unto them, leading away the hearts of many, causing them to lift up their heads in their wickedness, yea, leading away many women, and also men, to commit whoredomes— telling them that when a man was dead, that was the end thereof. (Alma 30:17-18)

The scripture immediately condemned Korihor for preaching personal responsibility. Personal responsibility is a control over the self, and the church wants possession of that. The faithful surrender their personal responsibilities to God in exchange for their own strength:

Now it came to pass that when Alma had said these words, that he clapped his hands upon all them who were with him. And behold, as he clapped his hands upon them, they were filled with the Holy Spirit.

And after that they did separate themselves one from another, taking no thought for themselves what they should eat, or what they should drink, or what they should put on.

And the Lord provided for them that they should hunger not, neither should they thirst; yea, and he also gave them strength, that they should suffer no manner of afflictions, save it were swallowed up in the joy of Christ. Now this was according to the prayer of Alma; and this because he prayed in faith. (Alma 31:36-38).

In this way, not only did the faithful lose responsibility over themselves, but they also lost credit for their own strength for afflictions by allowing God to claim it as His gift to them for their faith. The church also stole wisdom from its victims, (2 Ne. 15:21, 24). The following perspective is given against those who questioned the prophecies of Christ's birth in Jerusalem from across the Atlantic Ocean:

Nevertheless, the people began to harden their hearts, all save it were the most believing part of them, both of the Nephites and also of the Lamanites, and began to depend upon their own strength and upon their own wisdom, saying:

Some things they may have guessed right, among so many; but behold, we know that all these great and marvelous works cannot come to pass, of which has been spoken.

And they began to reason and to contend among themselves, saying:

That it is not reasonable that such a being as a Christ shall come; if so, and he be the Son of God, the Father of heaven and of earth, as it has been spoken, why will he not show himself unto us as well as unto them who shall be at Jerusalem?

But behold, we know that this is a wicked tradition, which has been handed down unto us by our fathers, to cause us that we should believe in some great and marvelous thing which should come to pass, but not among us, but in a land which is far distant, a land which we know not; therefore they can keep us in ignorance, for we cannot witness with our own eyes that they are true.

And they will, by the cunning and the mysterious arts of the evil one, work some great mystery which we cannot understand, which will keep us down to be servants to their words, and also servants unto them, for we depend upon them to teach us the word; and thus will they keep us in ignorance if we will yield ourselves unto them, all the days of our lives.

86

And many more things did the people imagine up in their hearts, which were foolish and vain; and they were much disturbed, for Satan did stir them up to do iniquity continually; yea, he did go about spreading rumors and contentions upon all the face of the land, that he might harden the hearts of the people against that which was good and against that which should come.

And notwithstanding the signs and the wonders which were wrought among the people of the Lord, and the many miracles which they did, Satan did get great hold upon the hearts of the people upon all the face of the land. (Hel. 16:15-23)

These doubters questioned the prophecies of Christ's birth in Jerusalem because the preachers had no evidence to show of it. At this time, nobody in the Americas had ever seen the continent across the ocean, and Jesus Christ had not yet visited the Americas. To these unbelievers, it was more possible that the testimony about the Son of God coming to earth was wrong than true. They found it more credible that the preachers were using false testimony to scam people into depending on them for information and life guidance. In response to the unbelief, the scripture affirms that these unbelievers became manipulated by the devil because of their questioning, and calls the unbelievers foolish and vain instead of attempting to understand and address their doubts.

Causing followers to believe that the devil has the ability to possess the unbeliever's mind is a powerful way to keep people from leaving the church. The devil is used to discourage the faithful from being influenced by unbelievers. By equating unbelief with evil character, the church alarms people of the evil of unbelievers, and this results in a cultivation of paranoia against them. The devil is given blame for every circumstance of disbelief or disobedience by his purposeful deception and control over people, as a way to enhance the reliability and effectiveness of this mechanism for paranoia. Any source that influences a person to disbelief is certainly of the devil, (Moro. 7:17). We know that God gives people only two options: either submit to Him, or be wicked, (2 Ne. 23:22), and all evil comes from the devil, (Moro. 7:12). All power of the wicked results from the devil killing people's spirits and taking them captive, (2 Ne. 2:27), therefore, all unbelievers are possessed by the devil. Worse than that, if God did not have mercy, all people would lose their spirits to possession by the devil:

Wherefore, it must needs be an infinite atonement—save it should be an infinite atonement this corruption could not put on incorruption. Wherefore, the first judgment which came upon man must needs have remained to an endless duration. And if so, this flesh must have laid down to rot and to crumble to its mother earth, to rise no more.

O the wisdom of God, his mercy and grace! For behold, if the flesh should rise no more our spirits must become subject to that angel who fell from before the presence of the Eternal God, and became the devil, to rise no more.

And our spirits must have become like unto him, and we become devils, angels to a devil, to be shut out from the presence of our God, and to remain with the father of lies, in misery, like unto himself; yea, to that being who beguiled our first parents, who transformeth himself nigh unto an angel of light, and stirreth up the children of men unto secret combinations of murder and all manner of secret works of darkness.

O how great the goodness of our God, who prepareth a way for our escape from the grasp of this awful monster; yea, that monster, death and hell, which I call the death of the body, and also the death of the spirit. (2 Ne. 9:7-10)

The extensive influence of the devil is shown by his ability to convince witnesses after just three years that a prophesied miracle of sustained daylight throughout a night either did not happen, or that it was some sort of deception, (3 Ne. 2:1-2). The devil has the ability to control people, (Alma 8:9). He is the author of all sin, (Hel. 6:18, 21, 29-30), and the father of all lies, (Ether 8:25), causing the believer to translate their own personal experiences, and observations of the behaviors of others sinning, as false proof of the devil's existence and power. All anger against the words of Nephi the son of Lehi comes from the devil, (2 Ne. 33:5). The devil is faulted for tricking people to go to Hell and for tricking people to believe that Hell does not exist, (2 Ne. 28:21-22). He is faulted for the torturing and killing of saints, (1 Ne. 13:5-6), and for administering a covenant to unite a gang against all righteousness, (3 Ne. 6:28). The Book of Mormon even provided testament of unbelievers who eventually confessed that they had been tricked by the devil, (Jacob 7:18; Alma 30:53). By providing these grounds for the faithful to develop paranoia against unbelievers, the church isolates its followers from being open to understanding the unbeliever. The church wants its followers to conclude that if all unbelievers are under the control of the devil, then their arguments against the church must all be tricks of the devil and not worth considering, and perhaps also dangerous to even hear. A demonstration for the faithful on how to do this was provided by Alma's response to Korihor's unbelief:

89

Behold, I know that thou believest, but thou art possessed with a lying spirit, and ye have put off the Spirit of God that it may have no place in you; but the devil has power over you, and he doth carry you about, working devices that he may destroy the children of God. (Alma 30:42)

In addition to the fear of Hell and of other punishments, by these teachings of the devil, the faithful are fearful of losing control over their own minds to him. Knowing that the devil has the power to influence people to unbelief directly within their hearts and minds, the faithful cling to the church in terror of losing control over themselves, because even with their faith, they are not immune from the devil's temptations. The faithful are urged to pray continually in order to stay safe from the devil, (Alma 34:39), teaching the faithful that they should never feel safe from this unless they are praying.

From the combination of the church's extensive enforcement of faith before pondering, and its prohibition of wisdom, followers are deprived of access to their own intellectual capabilities. Because the teachings of the church are not perfectly logical and because the believer has already concluded that the church is correct, the teachings that do not make sense add to the believer's personal experience of being unable to understand. The faithful therefore conclude that they are intellectually inadequate. When doubt is expressed against someone's ability, which in this case is communicated through the scriptures by prohibiting people from seeking wisdom, it has a negative effect on self-efficacy, (Baron, 1988). Low self-efficacy causes underperformance, and when a person remembers their previous experiences of inadequacy, those experiences further actuate underperformance, (Bandura, 1997).

Preachers within the testament who provide the believing reader with information and interpretation about the religion enable the believer to compare themselves to this esteemed artificial intelligence of the preachers. This comparison to a fictitious embodiment of flawless intellect could also add to the follower's feelings of inadequacy regardless of their normal intellectual ability, because in contrast with the spiritual success of the preachers within the testament, the efforts of the believer and of others they personally know within the church community have been unable to reach that same high level of esteem, even though they are told that if they only have faith that is strong enough, they can be like the saints, (Jacob 4:6).

Self-efficacy is generalized to different situations, (Bandura, 1997). Low self-efficacy deprives the bearer of the fullness of life, and of access to their own potential to succeed in general. By neglecting their full intellectual capabilities, these victims fail to reap the benefits of learning opportunities throughout their lives, and this state of underdevelopment retroactively contributes to their low self-efficacy as experiences of feeling inadequate. As a protection to this mechanism within the faith for those who are still seeking ways to be wise, the church curbs perseverance for wisdom by equating wisdom with fear, (Jacob 6:8-13), and promotes this false wisdom with the reward of happiness in the afterlife, (2 Ne. 9:43). This mechanism ensures that the believer will stay focused on the faith and will therefore be less likely to find true wisdom.

Low self-efficacy can cause people to assume that they are not fit to lead other church members as spiritual guides. If a person does not have the power of miracles, the flaw is with them for not believing well enough. To show how esteemed the preachers were in the Book of Mormon, Alma, the high priest and founder of the early Church of Christ, was the only person in his nation with the approval of God to bestow the authority to preach onto other people, and only men could be eligible, (Mosiah 23:17). Although not all, some of those who do believe that they are especially ideal candidates to preach in the Church of Christ today might characteristically shield themselves from reality, because of an inability to accept that they could possibly be intellectually inferior to the preceding preachers of the church, or unable to reach the fictitious perfection of faith shown by the testimony about those who had the power to perform miracles, (Morm. 8:24). These people use leadership positions to attempt to prove to themselves and others that they are just as great as the saints. Denial of reality reflects an inability to face it. It does not matter if the denial defends the actor against a true reality or not. If something is a reality according to the reasoning of the denier, then that denial against what that person actually believes alludes to their weakness. Church leaders like these need a constant supply of approval and admiration from others in order to sustain this denial that protects them from the reality they fear. Even if a believer became a preacher without this denial, in being appointed to this position, they gain reason to believe that, like those who were appointed by Alma, they have also been chosen by God, and can therefore be assured of the accuracy of their teachings. Leadership positions in service to the church offer an effective and functioning platform for manipulating victims, who are already primed for use by their faith. If the faithful members of the church view leaders like this as wise, or even chosen by God, they will listen in awe, believe them, and obey them, because these faithful believe that they were unable to understand what leaders like these seem to understand so well, and that they were unable to earn this same trust from God as leaders themselves.

The Book of Mormon cultivates and secures vulnerability into its followers by manufacturing insecure attachments. The concept of attachment styles in psychology describes a person's perceptions and expectations of their vulnerability to others and to themselves. People who have a secure attachment style trust that other people are generally not seeking to harm them, or if they are, the securely attached do not fear that those who are not trustworthy are dangerous to their self-dignity. The securely attached also trust and value themselves intrapersonally. Psychology recognizes three categories of insecure attachment. People who value themselves and trust themselves to maintain intrapersonal control well enough without help, yet feel generally untrusting and vulnerable interacting or attaching with others, are described as having the dismissive attachment style. These people are described as dismissive because their experiences have taught them that to ensure stability in their relationships, they should dismiss their own emotions, feelings, and opportunities for intimacy with others. They believe that it is generally not worth the effort to seek intimacy in relationships. Those who do not value themselves intrapersonally, yet feel generally trusting and safe enough attaching to others, have a preoccupied attachment. These people are described as preoccupied because since they struggle to love and trust themselves, yet trust others, they are preoccupied with seeking reassurance and love from others. The most complicated insecure attachment type is known as fearful-avoidant attachment. These people have both low self-esteem and experience high vulnerability in attachments with others. Like the preoccupied, the fearful-avoidant is also mentally preoccupied with seeking reassurance and love from others, yet at the same time, like the dismissive type, they are dismissive of attachment with others because they do not generally trust that they will be safe in those relationships. They may also numb their own feelings and emotions like the dismissive type. To show how these insecure attachments are manufactured, we must examine how the Book of Mormon provides each component.

Low self-esteem is a component in preoccupied and fearful-avoidant attachments. A person with Low self-esteem does not love themselves unconditionally, if they love themselves at all. Low self-esteem is required in order to have a relationship with God, (2 Ne. 9:42). We are worth nothing, (Mosiah 4:11; Hel. 12:7), and recognizing this is an indication of holiness, (Alma 26:12). God requires that we are submissive and that we endure long suffering, (Alma 7:23), and that we must fast, and give our whole souls away to Him, (Omni 1:26). Humility is promoted as tolerance and endurance through persecutions and afflictions without reviling against them, (3 Ne. 6:13). Our wrongs against God are too severe for forgiveness or self-improvement without redemption by the Son of God, (2 Ne. 2:5-6; Alma 34:9-10). God does not want a relationship with us without approval and bloody sacrifice from His son Jesus Christ, (2 Ne. 2:8). We will only be worthy of God through the Son of God, because our debt to God is eternal, (Mosiah 2:23-24). We are unable to be virtuous people in control of ourselves without imitating Jesus and receiving baptism, (2 Ne. 31:16-17). Unless we submit to the faith of the church, we are damning ourselves, (Mosiah 3:18), meaning that when we experience doubts, we are self-harming. Self-harm teaches the individual that they are not valuable, lowering self-esteem. The Anti-Nephi-Lehies were praised for making covenants to allow enemies to take their lives without resistance, as defending their lives against them would be sinful, (Alma 24:18-19), and they were not allowed to change their minds later for a noble cause of self-defense, (Alma 53:13-15). Believers gathered together praying that God will throw them to the enemy if they fall into transgression, (Alma 46:22), instead of praying that God help them back to righteousness if they were to transgress. Also, by prohibiting wisdom and thought before faith, the individual is taught that they cannot ever be trusted to think alone. We cannot have control over our own minds because unless we allow God to control us, the devil will, (2 Ne. 9:7-10). Imagine being so worthless that you are never permitted to have control over your own mind by your own creator. A mind that cannot be trusted to obey the spirit abiding within it is more difficult to value.

The scripture condemns people from giving love and attention to themselves in their lifestyles. Self-love is slandered as an illusion against our nothingness as children of God. It is labeled "pride", and it is interpreted as disrespectful toward anything good. Pride, meaning a feeling of satisfaction or thrill in one's success or from one's perceived ability to succeed, is not always delusional nor harmful, nor disrespectful toward others. In scripture, pride is deemed dangerous for the soul, (Jacob 2:16). Individuals, cultures, and civilizations who are prideful are accused of aggression against God, and destruction is promised against them, (1 Ne. 11:36;

Hel. 7:26). Pride is a definitive indication of evil and alliance with the devil, (2 Ne. 26:10; 28:12-15; 3 Ne. 6:15). Even saints are unworthy of pride, (Mosiah 23:11). Seeking immediate pleasure is also deemed dangerous:

Yea, and there shall be many which shall say: Eat, drink, and be merry, for tomorrow we die; and it shall be well with us.

And there shall also be many which shall say: Eat, drink, and be merry; nevertheless, fear God— he will justify in committing a little sin; yea, lie a little, take the advantage of one because of his words, dig a pit for thy neighbor; there is no harm in this; and do all these things, for tomorrow we die; and if it so be that we are guilty, God will beat us with a few stripes, and at last we shall be saved in the kingdom of God.

Yea, and there shall be many which shall teach after this manner, false and vain and foolish doctrines, and shall be puffed up in their hearts, and shall seek deep to hide their counsels from the Lord; and their works shall be in the dark.

And the blood of the saints shall cry from the ground against them.

Yea, they have all gone out of the way; they have become corrupted. (2 Ne. 28:7-11)

Seeking immediate pleasure can be unhealthy if it proceeds from failure to self-discipline. Unregulated procrastination or dismissal of more important work or cause for the sake of merriment can harm the soul. However, it is not wrong simply to have fun for your own sake. Attending to your interests is important because it communicates to the spirit that she is valuable. Avoiding all pleasures as if they are evil can harm self-esteem. The Book of Mormon may be enforcing fear or disdain of immediate pleasure as a way

96

to limit the believer to depend on the church as the only source of happiness and importance.

Because they do not see value in themselves, the preoccupied person hungers for reassurance from other people, but that hunger also remains unsatiated regardless of these efforts because it is never enough to change their low self-esteem. Remembering how intermittent reinforcement schedules work can help us understand how these people can be stubbornly preoccupied with seeking reassurance from others because it is inconsistency in attachments that causes their insecurity and persistence. This component of inconsistency is provided by all the rewards that are offered for faith within the scripture in combination with all of God's threats of rejection and examples of His abandonment of people. It can be derived from God's apparent inconsistency in answering prayer and His unequal treatment of people both in giving special privileges to some and placing others at a disadvantage in comparison to those born under the church or those that receive more mercy. Among many other examples discussed previously, chosen disciples of Jesus were protected from the temptations of the devil before the afterlife, but nobody else mentioned in the Book of Mormon received this privilege, (3 Ne. 28:36, 39). As for placing some people at a disadvantage, people were discriminated against before they were born, such as the children of the Lamanites who were cursed with dark skin and barred from the mercy of God, (Alma 3:14). The preoccupied person feels that security of their relationships are unpredictable because of their experience with inconsistency in attachments, and this is what drives them to seek reassurance endlessly because they expect failure in relationships from minuscule disturbances. Knowing that the scripture promotes hope by saying that God tests the faith of His people, creating preoccupied attachments may be part of the same agenda. It can be difficult enough for the believer to identify patterns in God's behavior that they might not know when to expect His mercy and when to expect His delay, dismissal, or punishing. This is a source of insecurity and pain that drives people to persistently seek reassurance from God, since they hope that they can receive the reassurance they crave at least some of the time.

Dismissive attachment is created from discomfort in bonding with others as well as emotional neglect within the self. With the paranoia the church breeds against unbelievers, a stubborn distrust arises against people. The devil's ease of power over the individual provides the dismissive person with the component of vulnerability to others. God's belittling of human dignity also contributes to the believer's distrust against both unbelievers and believers, because God's perspective is interpreted as factual and ideal. Knowing God's perfect justice and equality can cause this distrust because of the huge percentage of people who are unbelievers. All of those unbelieving people have dismissed God and goodness, showing their lack of concern for what is most important, and therefore, cannot be good candidates for intimacy. To cause emotional neglect, God gives us reasons to distrust Him with our emotions and feelings. We are enemies to God before we have the ability to do anything, (Mosiah 3:19). God's forgiveness is not genuine because He is willing to take it away, (Mosiah 4:12). To God, we are not eligible to think for ourselves. Unless we submit to God under duress of the threat of eternal hell, we are worthless to Him, therefore, nothing we think or feel is relevant. God does not care enough to help the unbelievers or answer their questions, but punishes them instead. He uses us and our sins for His own agenda, (Mosiah 21:3-4, Alma 42:5). He also neglects those who submit to Him because He delays answering mighty prayer, and He only allows a select few to hear His voice, have supernatural powers, intellect to preach, and miraculous protection from physical and spiritual harm. The rest of us who have not experienced these privileges must be so far from achieving control over our thoughts and feelings that we are unworthy of having this relationship with God, even though this relationship would cost God nothing due to His infinite power and virtue. God is not interested in our opinions, feelings, nor our emotions, but only in our actions. In disaster, He spared the lives of the more righteous over the wicked, and seemed to expect their gratitude for this, while remaining entirely indifferent towards their valid feelings of grief for the loss of the quality of their lives, (3 Ne. 9:13). By doing this, God either showed that He believes people to be so shallow that they find greater gratitude in anatomical life rather than in the quality of living, or that He did not care about how these people felt at all, and that He was only saving the lives of the more righteous in order to threaten them into compliance after punishing them with utter despair. God also shows that our intentions do not matter, but only our actions, such as when He declared that He would no longer accept burnt offerings as an expression of worship, (3 Ne. 9:19). By His indifference, God influences people to keep at a distance away from Him. Desiring to secure and preserve their delicate attachment with God from this distance, followers then focus more on impressing Him with their actions, accomplishments, and stubborn faith rather than communicating with Him intimately about their thoughts. Because God knows all things, the only way to hide thoughts and feelings from God is to dismiss or destroy them. In addition to this, suffering is promoted by the scripture. God's people are expected to tolerate afflictions, (2 Ne. 9:18; Jacob 1:8), quietly accept mistreatment, and do nothing in response to mistreatment except to wait patiently for peace to come, (Alma 34:40-41), which might not come on its own until after death. If the believer's feelings and emotions harm their attachment with God, they learn to dismiss them and eventually develop alexithymia, which is a character trait of an inability to identify and describe feelings and emotions as well as a lack of awareness for the connection of these feelings to bodily responses. The fearful-avoidant person knows that suffering secures their bond with God, and because they are also preoccupied with receiving reassurance from outside sources, without other ways to secure this, they may seek opportunities to suffer. This person could potentially employ this harmful attachment mechanism to any circumstance of emotional insecurity in their life.

God's infinite power has access to every aspect, person, and natural occurrence in the believer's life. Through this perspective, these manufactured insecure attachments extend beyond church-related activity and captivate the believer's life and identity at all times, and constrain their potential. Parents and caregivers within the church who want the best for their children take examples from God's behavior and the scriptures, and may naturally cause insecure attachments in their children. A natural insecure attachment formed in childhood through parenting would not be rectified simply by leaving the church.

By maximizing control over the victim's relationship with their own money, thoughts, personal responsibilities, spiritual strengths, exposure to unbelievers and their perspectives, exposure to doubts, intellect, self-efficacy, self-love, feelings, and emotions, the grasp of the church on its victims is extremely thorough, extending to any possible situation in the victim's life, preventing the victim's escape from the grasp of the church as effectively as possible. If the church of Christ is truly in alignment with the Book of Mormon, it is spiritually hazardous and should be rejected as a source of guidance. Consider why God created you and what He wants for you. Is it perfectly the same as what the true church seeks for you?

Conclusion

Salvation

Because all beliefs require faith, any theory could be true. To most accurately determine which possibility is the most likely truth, we must employ the law of parsimony. This is the principle that whichever theory contains the least amount of assumption will reflectively have the most evidence and require the least amount of faith. You may have read certain prosecuting arguments within this book and thought to yourself that my examination is flawed. You should not ignore thoughts like this, nor should you ignore your doubts against the church. Instead, suspend your fears in the privacy of your mind for a moment, remember your perfect, loving God, and focus on the math. considering all explanations for a given topic, think: which possible truth requires the least amount of assumption, or faith, to be believed? No single isolated doubt nor evidence should determine a verdict on a possible truth. All prosecutions and defenses should be considered in totality to determine the answers to the bigger questions, in this case: "Is the Book of Mormon truthful?", and, "Is the Book of Mormon a good spiritual guide?"

While maintaining authority over emotions, it is important that you do not immediately dismiss your own mental experiences in favor or dismissal of any theory. Instead, recognize that your experiences were real, and therefore, are valid to consider, whether they are supportive for, or against the theory you are testing, and apply the law of parsimony as the judge of your own courtroom. Remember, for example, all your prayers that God answered, all those He seemed to ignore, all the miracles He performed for you, and all the anguishes He abandoned you to. Consider opposite explanations for God's decisions in each experience, even if you do not believe or perhaps do not like some of those explanations. Compare the behaviors of both believing and unbelieving characters in the scriptures to your interactions with believing and unbelieving characters in your own life. Consider your experiences in totality with whatever other evidence you have. Compare your experiences to the teachings of the church. If you come to an ultimate conclusion which was thoroughly considered and entirely your own, you will not have to find yourself burdened with those same doubts ever again. A great benefit of the law of parsimony is that you do not have to know everything or be an expert to make a conclusion for yourself. You simply work with the information that you have, and as you receive new information, you can simply reevaluate for the most reliable conclusion.

Once you reach your verdict, remember to recognize your feelings that you have temporarily set aside for the trial. Different people will experience different feelings in similar circumstances, but any real feelings are valid. If you find yourself firmer in your faith and perhaps angered with my cynicism against it, your feelings are valid, and you are welcome to enjoy the freedom and peace from future doubt with a strengthened relationship with God. If you find yourself fearful and uncertain, know that acknowledging uncertainty is honest and valid. Uncertainty is not a failure. It is merely a condition. Continue to seek answers, and maintain authority over that discomfort so that you can allow truth to restore peace in your mind. If you find that your faith in the church of Christ has crumbled, and you feel scared, sad, manipulated, or alone, know that your feelings are entirely normal, valid, and understandable. One of the most burdening emotions following a crisis of Christian faith is the real fear of being abandoned by God and condemned to Hell forever if you find yourself wrong after death. An important thing to remember for this and any other insecurity you may feel from rejecting the church is that you can truly fully resolve them, but that you must be patient with yourself. A masterpiece is not created overnight. Progress is gradual and difficult to notice, and there may be many setbacks along the way. Excellence is not determined based on lack of insecurities, but on how you respond to their presence. To address the fear of Hell, in your logical mind, remember your perfect, loving God. Imagine that you are God, with infinite power and perfect love. Imagine this God burning His own children in a prison of the most extreme misery, forever and ever. Recognize the immense amount of justification this reasoning would require, and take comfort in your new, more plausible faith in your loving Father. Solidify that plausibility in your consciousness now, so that in times of spiritual fatigue, you will remember your logical certainty, and grant it authority over your emotions.

If your doubts have been defeated along with your religious faith, know that allowing yourself to change your opinion is not a weakness, but a power of spiritual access. You have gained access to a new perspective which was hidden from you, and from that, you can develop parts of your identity that you could not touch before. Although you may never forget how to think of yourself or humanity negatively, with a new, stronger identity, you will no longer have to use your old perspective. At the end of your journey for Truth, if you happen to find yourself in the same place I did when I left Christianity, you will discover that instead of losing God, He has remained with you, and you have grown closer to Him than you ever were before. Love yourself, because your powerful, loving God Is, right here within you, united with you, connected with you through the Way, the Truth, and the Life, forever, and no one comes to salvation and eternal happiness except through the power of God.

References

Alberdi, M.T., and J. L. Prado. 1993. Review of the genus *Hippidion* Owen, 1869 (Mammalia: Perissodactyla) from the Pleistocene of South America. *Zoological Journal of the Linnean Society, 108(1),* 1-22.

Anderson, C., Lepper, M. and Ross, L., 1980. Perseverance of social theories: The role of explanation in the persistence of discredited information. *Journal of Personality and Social Psychology,* 39(6), pp. 1037-1049.

Avilla, L. dos, Graciano Figueiredo, A. M., Kinoshita, A., Bertoni-Machado, C., Mothé, D., Asevedo, L., Baffa, O., & Dominato, V. H. (2013). Extinction of a gomphothere population from Southeastern Brazil: Taphonomic, paleoecological and chronological remarks. *Quaternary International,* *305,* 85–90. https://doi.org/10.1016/j.quaint.2012.09.015

Bandura, A. (1997). *Self-efficacy: The exercise of control.* W H Freeman/Times Books/Henry Holt & Co.

Bandura, A. (2016). *Moral disengagement how people do harm and live with themselves.* New York, NY: Worth Publishers, Macmillan learning.

Baron, R. A. (1988). Negative effects of destructive criticism: Impact on conflict, self-efficacy, and task performance. *Journal of Applied Psychology*, 73, 199-207.

Epley, N., & Dunning, D. (2000). Feeling "holier than thou": Are self-serving assessments produced by errors in self- or social prediction? *Journal of Personality and Social Psychology, 79*(6), 861–875.

Ferster, C. B., & Skinner, B. F. (1997). Fixed Ratio. In Schedules of reinforcement. Acton, MA: Copley Pub. Group. (Original work published 1957).

Gershoff, E.T. (2002). Corporal punishment by parents and associated child behaviors and experiences: A meta-analytic and theoretical review. *Psychological Bulletin*, 128, 539-579.

Haile, J., Froese, D., MacPhee, R., Roberts, R., Arnold, L., Reyes, A., Rasmussen, M., Nielsen, R., Brook, B., Robinson, S., Demuro, M., Gilbert, M., Munch, K., Austin, J., Cooper, A., Barnes, I., Möller, P. and Willerslev, E., 2009. Ancient DNA reveals late survival of mammoth and horse in interior Alaska. Proceedings of the National Academy of Sciences, 106(52), pp. 22352-22357.

Hamlin JK, Wynn K, Bloom P. Social evaluation by preverbal infants. Nature. 2007; 450:557–559.

Hanks, P., Hardcastle, K., & Hodges, F. (2007). *A dictionary of first names* (2nd ed.). Oxford: Oxford University Press.

Harmon-Jones, E., & Mills, J. (1999). *An introduction to cognitive dissonance theory and an overview of current perspectives on the theory.* In E. Harmon-Jones (Ed.), *Cognitive dissonance: Progress on a pivotal theory in psychology* (p. 3–21). Washington, DC: American Psychological Association.

Heider, F. (1946). Attitudes and Cognitive Organization. *The Journal of Psychology, 21*(1), 107–112. https://doi.org/10.1080/00223980.1946.9917275

Meltzer, D. J., & Mead, J. I. (1983). The Timing of Late Pleistocene Mammalian Extinctions in North America. *Quaternary Research, 19*(1), 130–135.

Prado, J., Sánchez, B. and Alberdi, M., 2011. Ancient feeding ecology inferred from stable isotopic evidence from fossil horses in South America over the past 3 Ma. *BMC ecology,* 11(1), P.15.

Regan, D. T., & Fazio, R. (1977). On the consistency between attitudes and behavior: Look to the method of attitude formation. *Journal of Experimental Social Psychology, 13*(1), 28-45. doi:10.1016/0022-1031(77)90011-7

Sanchez, G., Holliday, V. T., Gaines, E. P., Arroyo-Cabrales, J., Martinez-Taguena, N., Kowler, A., Lange, T., Hodgins, G. W., Mentzer, S. M., & Sanchez-Morales, I. (2014). Human (Clovis)-gomphothere (Cuvieronius sp.) association 13,390 calibrated yBP in Sonora, Mexico. *Proceedings of the National Academy of Sciences,*

111(30), 10972–10977.
https://doi.org/10.1073/pnas.1404546111

Schurr, T. G., and S. T. Sherry. 2004. Mitochondrial
DNA and Y chromosome diversity and the
peopling of the Americas: evolutionary and
demographic evidence. *American Journal of
Human Biology* 16:420-439.

The Society of Saint Pius X, South-West District, Inc.
(2020, April 27). *General statistics about the
SSPX*. District of the USA.
https://sspx.org/en/general-statistics-aboutsspx.

Stein, N., & Muehlbauer, G. J. (Eds.). (2018). *The
Barley Genome*. SPRINGER.

Vartanyan, S. L., Arslanov, K. A., Karhu, J. A.,
Possnert, G., & Sulerzhitsky, L. D. (2008).
Collection of radiocarbon dates on the mammoths
(Mammuthus Primigenius) and other genera of
Wrangel Island, northeast Siberia, Russia.
Quaternary Research, 70(1), 51-59.

Veltre, D. W., Yesner, D. R., Crossen, K. J., Graham,
R. W., & Coltrain, J. B. (2008). Patterns of
faunal extinction and paleoclimatic change
from mid-Holocene mammoth and polar bear
remains, Pribilof Islands, Alaska. *Quaternary
Research, 70*(1), 40–50.
https://doi.org/https://doi.org/10.1016/j.yqres.

Warneken, F., 2013. Young children proactively
remedy unnoticed accidents. Cognition, 126(1),
pp.101-108.

Made in the USA
Middletown, DE
25 November 2021

53013597R00066